THE FEAR FACTOR

The Living as a Christian Series

Basic Christian Maturity

Growing in Faith
  Steve Clark
Knowing God's Will
  Steve Clark
Decision to Love
  Ken Wilson
God First
  Ken Wilson
Sons and Daughters of God
  Ken Wilson
Growing Closer to God
  Tom Gryniewicz

Overcoming Obstacles to Christian Living

How to Repair the Wrong You've Done
  Ken Wilson
Getting Free
  Bert Ghezzi

The Emotions

Facing Your Feelings
  Bert Ghezzi
The Angry Christian
  Bert Ghezzi
The Self-Image of a Christian
  Mark Kinzer
Living with a Clear Conscience
  Mark Kinzer
The Fear Factor
  Jim McFadden

Christian Character

Strength under Control
  John Keating
How to Become the Person You Were Meant to Be
  Peter Williamson

Personal Relationships

Taming the Tongue
  Mark Kinzer

**Bert Ghezzi and Peter Williamson
General Editors**

The Fear Factor

Everyone Has It. You Can Master It.

Jim McFadden

SERVANT BOOKS
Ann Arbor, Michigan

Copyright © 1983 by Jim McFadden

Published by Servant Books
        P.O. Box 8617
        Ann Arbor, Michigan 48107

Cover photo by John B. Leidy © 1983 Servant Publications.
Book design by John B. Leidy

Scripture quotations are from the *Revised Standard Version* copyrighted 1946, 1952 © 1971, 1973 by the Division of Christian Education of the National Council of the Churches of Christ in the U.S.A.

Printed in the United States of America
ISBN 0-89283-159-6

Contents

Series Introduction / 7

1. What Fear Is / 13
2. What Are You Afraid Of? / 25
3. Fear—Good or Bad? / 39
4. Marks of the Christian:
   Confidence, Boldness, and Courage / 59
5. Standing on Solid Rock / 75
6. The Shield of Faith / 87
7. Looking Reality in the Eye / 103
8. Tilt the Odds in Your Favor / 125
9. Direct Attack on Problem Fears / 139
10. A Fighting Spirit / 159

SERIES INTRODUCTION

Living as a Christian

IN HUMAN TERMS, it is not easy to decide to follow Jesus Christ and to live our lives as Christians. Jesus requires that we surrender our selves to him, relinquish our aspirations for our lives, and submit our will to God. Men and women have never been able to do this easily; if we could, we wouldn't need a savior.

Once we accept the invitation and decide to follow Jesus, a new set of obstacles and problems assert themselves. We find that we are often ignorant about what God wants of us as his sons and daughters. For example, what does it mean practically to obey the first commandment—to love God with our whole mind, heart, and strength? How can we know God's will? How do we love people we don't like? How does being a Christian affect what we do with our time and money? What does it mean "to turn the other cheek"? In these areas—and many others—it is not easy to understand exactly what God wants.

Even when we do know what God wants, it can be quite difficult to apply his teaching to our daily lives. Questions abound. How do we find time to pray regularly? How do we repair a relationship with someone we have wronged or who has wronged us? How do we handle unruly emotional reactions? These are examples of perplexing questions about the application of Christian teaching to our daily lives.

Furthermore, we soon discover that Christians have enemies—the devil outside and the flesh within. Satan tempts us to sin; our inner urges welcome the temptation, and we find our will to resist steadily eroding.

Finally, we must overcome the world. We are trying to live in an environment that is hostile toward what Christians believe and how they live and friendly toward those who believe and do the opposite. The world in which we live works on our Christian resolve in many subtle ways. How much easier it is to think and act like those around us! How do we persevere?

There is a two-fold answer to these questions: To live successfully as Christians, we need both grace and wisdom. Both are freely available from the Lord to those who seek him.

As Christians we live by grace. The very life of God works in us as we try to understand God's teaching, apply it to our lives, and overcome the forces that would turn us aside from our chosen path. The grace we need is always there. The Lord is with us always, and the supply of his grace is inexhaustible.

Yet grace works with wisdom. Christians must *learn* a great deal about how to live according to

God's will. We must study God's word in scripture, listen to Christian teaching, and reflect on our own experience and the experience of others. Many Christians today lack this kind of wisdom. This is the need which the *Living as a Christian* series is designed to meet.

The book you are reading is part of a series of books intended to help Christians apply the teaching of scripture to their lives. The authors of *Living as a Christian* books are pastoral leaders who have given this teaching in programs of Christian formation in various Christian communities. The teaching has stood the test of time. It has already helped many people grow as faithful servants of the Lord. We decided it was time to make this teaching available in book form.

All the *Living as a Christian* books seek to meet the following criteria:

Biblical. The teaching is rooted in scripture. The authors and editors maintain that scripture is the word of God, and that it ought to determine what Christians believe and how they live.

Practical. The purpose of the series is to offer down-to-earth advice about living as a Christian.

Relevant. The teaching is aimed at the needs we encounter in our daily lives—at home, in school, on the job, in our day-to-day relationships.

Brief and Readable. We have designed the series for busy people from a wide variety of backgrounds. Each of the authors presents profound Christian truths as simply and clearly as possible, and illustrates those truths by examples drawn from personal experience.

Integrated. The books in the series comprise a unified curriculum on Christian living. They do not present differing views, but rather they take a consistent approach.

The format of the series makes it suitable for both individual and group use. The books in *Living as a Christian* can be used in such group settings as Sunday school classes, adult education programs, prayer groups, classes for teen-agers, women's groups, and as a supplement to Bible study.

The *Living as a Christian* series is divided into several sets of books, each devoted to a different aspect of Christian living. This book, *The Fear Factor,* is part of a set covering the emotions in the Christian life. The nature of modern society forces us to be more concerned about our emotions than our Christian ancestors had to be. Not that they were unemotional. Ironically, they were more expressive of their emotions than most of us are. But nowadays we look at our emotions differently, and the instability of relationships and pressures of modern life introduce some new problems. *The Fear Factor* and other books in this set present a practical, scripturally based strategy for emotional health.

The editors dedicate the *Living as a Christian* series to Christian men and women everywhere who have counted the cost and decided to follow Jesus Christ as his disciples.

> Bert Ghezzi and Peter Williamson
> General Editors

ONE

What Fear Is

Down the street lives a guy named Charlie. Chicken Charlie they call him. He loves to garden but gave it up some years ago because he was afraid of getting skin cancer from exposure to the sun. Now he stays indoors most of the time and worries about falling victim to a vitamin deficiency. He doesn't go camping because he's afraid of being bitten by mosquitos and doesn't go golfing because he might get hit by a ball. At work he has carefully chosen a noncompetitive and unchallenging job to protect himself from the possibility of failure. He has lots of friends that he likes a great deal but is not so sure that they like him in return. Charlie is very careful. He looks both ways at least three times before he crosses the street, bundles up carefully in case of cold weather, tries not to inhale deeply when in crowds because he might catch some disease, and has a bomb shelter in his basement. Chicken Charlie is likely to live a long but miserable life.

A guy much the opposite of Charlie used to live next door, but he's been gone for some years now.

14 *The Fear Factor*

Fearless Freddie was his name. By the age of five he had worn out eleven tricycles by crashing them into the concrete foundation of his home just for the thrill of it. At the age of seven he ate three night-crawlers and a toad on a fifty-cent bet. At sixteen he dived off a ninety-foot cliff and spent three months in the hospital recuperating from a compression fracture of several vertebrae. Fearless Freddie was real sociable, popular in school, and excelled at sports. At the age of twenty-three he tried to be the last one to cross a drawbridge which was being raised and drove his new Camaro down the smokestack of an oceangoing freighter. You don't meet many guys like Freddie. Maybe that's because guys like Freddie, like Fearless Freddie himself, don't live very long.

I know another guy, very different from Charlie and Freddie, whose name is Balanced Billy. Last summer, while on vacation in the countryside, Billy took a shortcut through a field and was chased by an angry bull. He took one look at the sharp horns and thundering hoofs, was scared nearly out of his socks, and set a new personal record for the hundred yard dash. He vaulted the nearest fence to safety. On another occasion Billy was taking his younger brother for a walk when a very aggressive German Shepherd challenged them. He felt fear rising within him but stood his ground, picked up a large stick, and backed up the dog. In his early teens, Balanced Billy moved to a new school and at first felt very shy and out of place. Nevertheless, he extended himself, made new friends, joined in activities, and soon got to feel very much at home. Throughout his life Billy has done a lot of different things, taken reasonable risks, learned to enjoy himself, and will probably live to a reasonable old age while having plenty of fun.

What Charlie had too much of and Freddie too little of, Billy seems to have working just right in his life. It's what we call fear. Too much fear, working in the wrong way, keeps Chicken Charlie in misery and bondage. Not enough fear led to a premature end to Fearless Freddie. In Billy's life, fear is something to be dealt with—sometimes overcome, other times responded to with common sense—but overall he gets along well with it and probably couldn't cope with life without it.

Every normal human being experiences fear from time to time. It's a part of our basic human makeup which serves a useful purpose in our lives. Fear rises within us as a reaction to danger. It equips us to respond to threatening situations. If an enemy attacks us or our house catches fire or the brakes fail in our car or a serious disease overtakes us, a normal and healthy response is fear. Many things in life are genuinely dangerous to us and ought to cause a fear reaction within us. But if we are afraid of things that aren't really dangerous, or react in wrong ways to proper fears, then we can say that we have a problem in this area of our lives. If we do have such a problem we can also say that the Lord wants to change us so that we can become fully mature and free Christian men and women.

The way that fear works in human life has changed a great deal as the centuries have gone by. When the Old Testament talks about fear, it usually refers to fear of very concrete, objective, physical dangers—obvious things that confront people's lives. Israelites living in a village were afraid of their enemies. They faced the possibility that a band of Midianites would march upon them, burn their houses, kill their kinfolk, and take away their crops and livestock. There was real physical danger in their lives—famine, pestilence, robbers—and fear was an appropriate response to it. People in modern technological society, however, face fewer of these fears. The main type of fear which people have to deal with today is social fear.

We probably have more time and energy available to devote to developing social fear than the ancient Israelites since we don't have to put so much of it into coping with the kinds of objective physical dangers typical of Old Testament times. But something else has changed as well. God created us as social beings; we need to be involved in a well-balanced set of stable human relationships. This need was fulfilled far better in the stable traditional societies of the past (like the society of Old Testament times) than it is in the rapidly changing, depersonalized society of today. The normal pattern of human relationships that was intended in God's plan for man has been seriously disrupted, with the result that people today are often left prey to a wide range of social fears. Instead of fear of famine or raid by a neighboring tribe, the student or factory worker or housewife of today is much more likely to have to cope with the fear of not being liked, accepted, or understood.

I have known people who were fairly certain in their own minds—although objectively dead wrong—that they were not liked by anyone. If you pause and think for a minute, you can probably remember a number of people you have known who were like this. I have seen it in young boys and girls who were still developing their foundation of self-confidence for life. But I have also seen it as a continuing lifelong curse in both men and women of much older ages. It is often somewhat skillfully disguised by a phony confident or aggressive manner or by excessive dedication to achievement. Sad to say, though, it's anything but an uncommon condition. Perhaps you are in this condition yourself.

Probably a majority of people would say that they are liked by some people—perhaps by quite a few. Their fear of not being liked, accepted, or understood focuses more specifically on certain very important people in their lives—parents, someone that they want very badly to have as a special friend, the boss at work, or classmates at school. Usually our fear of being disliked by such people is based upon something we dislike in ourselves that we believe other people will be turned off by. It could be our big nose or bad complexion or body shape. Maybe we don't like the sound of our voice or can't afford to dress as stylishly as our friends and so are afraid that we won't fit in. Some people are crushed by the fears that build upon these self-concerns, while others with the same characteristics see them as no handicap at all. Many people are afraid of making mistakes—on the job or in social situations. They are sure that they are going to botch something and that other people will see it and reject them because of it. Educational level, I.Q., race, beliefs, culture—all can be a basis for the fear that other people will not like or accept us.

Another category of fears that is a huge problem for many people today is what might be called "anxious concerns." These, like social fears, are fed by powerful forces that operate in modern life, especially the heavy demand for performance, the deluge of information from media sources, and the high rate of change in almost every area of life. There is a difference between proper concern and anxious concern. Proper concern leads us to take an appropriate action when something that we have a responsibility for needs attention. Anxious concern is a fearful stewing over a situation that we can't possibly change or that we have already done all we can to set straight. Parents, for example, often worry too much about whether their children are doing well enough in school. A surprisingly large number of perfectly healthy people are extremely anxious over their health. Others fret about both their personal finances (which they could probably do a great deal to manage better) and the global economy (which they can't do anything about at all). Still others bear a destructive burden of anxiety over social injustice, poverty, warfare, crime, and immorality. We can each make a small individual contribution to solve such large problems, but we cannot possibly take on the full burden for them.

We are all sinners ourselves, and certain basic disorders prevail in our world because it is alienated from God. As a result, many of the experiences that shape our emotional patterns are anything but what God intended. We are exposed to a certain amount of wrong teaching or bad example that shapes the way fear works within us; our own confusion, cowardice, or self-concern may block healthy emotional development; and the Evil One misses no opportunity to throw obstacles in the path we follow toward Christian maturity. It's little wonder then that this thing called fear—intended by God to protect us and serve us in life—often is more of a burden than a benefit. When fear isn't working right in our lives, it can cause great misery, physical stress leading to illness, and wrong behavior. But the Lord has a remedy for everything that has gone wrong in our lives and that misshapes our emotional responses. Whether the problem stems from something done to us or something we ourselves have done, the Lord has some means, either natural or miraculous, through which he will work to free us from bondage to fear.

We can better manage fear and better cooperate with God's action in freeing us from fear problems if we understand what fear is, where it comes from, and how it works in our lives. Let's dispel some of the mystery about fear.

The simplest experience of fear is an internal state or emotional feeling that comes as a response to danger. Some of this feeling comes from physiological changes in our bodies when we are faced by danger. These changes are caused by our nervous system and by glands that secrete special chemicals that enter our bloodstream. The feeling of fear also comes from our knowledge of the danger we are in and its possible consequences to us. So fear is partly a matter of nerves, partly a matter of glands, and partly a matter of thoughts. We don't usually sort these three things out, but just experience one overall feeling that we refer to as "fear."

In war time, when a ship on patrol sights the enemy, general quarters is sounded. The crew drop whatever else they may be doing and scramble to their duty stations. The normal activites of life come to a halt so that the ship can be prepared for battle. Guns are readied, the ship moves to full speed, lookouts are doubled. The hatches are battened down, and watertight compartment doors are closed so that possible damage to the ship can be contained. Repair crews are alerted and take their stations. Something of a revolution takes place inside the ship to prepare it to meet the danger posed by the enemy.

Much the same thing happens within the human body when danger threatens. The nervous system goes on full alert, and adrenaline pours into the bloodstream to mobilize all bodily resources. The heartbeat increases in rate and strength to carry more oxygen to the muscles. The liver releases stored sugar. The sugar and oxygen produce the combustion in the body that provides energy for fight or flight. The spleen contracts and releases more red blood cells, which help carry more oxygen. Breathing deepens and bronchial tubes dilate—additional means of getting more oxygen into the blood. More blood is routed to the muscles and brain where it is needed; less goes to the skin and internal organs. The pupils of the eyes dilate, increasing the efficiency of our vision. The ability of blood to coagulate is increased, and special cells called lymphocytes, which help repair damaged tissues, are released into the bloodstream. All this happens in a matter of seconds or minutes. Our heart pounds, our breathing deepens, and we feel a tightness in the pit of our stomach. Oftentimes we speak of somebody being "pale with fear." These reactions are a result of the rerouting of blood from where it's less needed to where it's most needed to deal with danger. They prepare the body for fight or flight, depending on the particular danger.

Still another response—a more common reaction in animals than in human beings—is to freeze in a state of immobility. Probably most of us have experienced all three of these reactions at one time or another. We may have outfought or outrun a school bully, or crouched motionless in the bushes, hoping that we blended in well with the leaves, while he walked by in search of us.

The feelings of fear, then, are both a warning and a result of changes taking place within us which prepare us to deal more effectively with danger. You do not know your full physical capacity until you are really frightened. All these preparations increase strength and endurance far above normal levels. Men have been known to lift cars or other heavy objects off themselves or trapped victims under the influence of fear. You do not know how fast or how far you can run until you are chased by something or someone that really frightens you.

Sometimes fear persists and the body has to adapt to a continuing state of preparedness or resistance. Hormones are released that allow the body to use more complicated compounds in the sugars for fuel. More sugar is deposited in the liver. More changes take place in the blood vessels to sustain strenuous activity. But keeping up this state of preparedness for a long time eventually causes trouble. The body gradually loses its ability to repair damage and fight off disease. Physical problems like ulcers develop. Eventually, continual mobilization in response to fear interferes with such vital bodily functions as growth and reproduction.

Fear, therefore, is useful—but within limits. It triggers bodily responses to help us handle danger, but there are definite limits to the body's ability to sustain itself in the face of continuing danger. If you lived in a forest full of wolves, you might learn to avoid them or fight them off and live a long and successful life. On the other hand, even if the wolves didn't kill you directly, the stress of living in a constant state of fear might shorten your life by ten or twenty years. Today not many of us live in a forest full of real, old-fashioned wolves (the ones with the fur coats). However, many of us do live in cities or suburbs where we either successfully fight off the wolves of social, financial, and achievement fears, or else lead a life of misery running from them, perhaps mercifully shortened by the ravages of stress.

I have described what fear is and how it operates within us in terms of response to concrete physical dangers. The emotion of fear works much the same way in the case of social fears and anxious concerns. However, there are two important differences between physical and social fear. First, a concrete physical danger is much more likely to be a real danger than a social fear or an anxious concern. These latter fears may be based on real dangers, but are perhaps just as often based on imaginary ones. The second major difference is that we usually do something in the face of a concrete physical danger, while we commonly do nothing effective to resolve misery with social fears and anxious concerns. If a car swerves toward you, you jump out of the way; if you hear an explosion, you dive for cover; if a growling dog approaches you, you run as fast as you can. You may not do the right thing, but you will almost certainly do something. By contrast, many people plagued with social fears do nothing about them. They will go through life avoiding others, afraid to relate, living in miserable isolation. Intelligent people feel dumb, attractive people feel ugly, and skilled people feel clumsy. They are so bound by social fear that they can't form the relationships they desire.

The Lord has freedom for those burdened by social fears. Whether the defects are real or imagined—and not all of them are imagined—we can be loved and accepted, and free from fear.

TWO

What Are You Afraid Of?

LET'S EXPAND OUR UNDERSTANDING of fear some more. First we will consider the things that trigger fear, then look at the natural ways in which patterns of fear develop and are erased in our lives. These are the patterns which the power of God will reshape if we have difficulties with fear. To describe the kinds of events that trigger the fear reaction, I'm going to invent a story about one of the worst afternoon naps you could ever experience.

It's a warm summer Saturday, your day off. You stretch out on the lounge in the yard and drowsily soak up the sun. In a corner of the yard the kids are playing peacefully in the sandbox. Suddenly a loud explosion interrupts your dozing. You jump to your feet, heart pounding, knees shaking. The kids have built a large sand castle and just blasted it to bits with a firecracker. The noise was loud and sudden. It triggered the reaction of fear. Ah well, back to sleep.

Some time later you are awakened by a huffing sound and the sensation of hot moist breath upon your face. You open your eyes and go rigid with terror, for towering over you is a beast the likes of which you have never imagined. "It looked friendly, but I never saw anything like it before," you explain later. You didn't know the neighbors had bought a new dog. You had never seen an Irish elk hound before in your life. After a few minutes, your fears begin to subside for no better reason than that you've survived the early moments of the encounter. You notice that the elk hound's tail is wagging. He licks your face, novel but nice. The neighbor comes and apologetically takes his new dog home. You go back to sleep.

A little later you wake up thirsty and reach for a cold drink in the ice chest beside your lounge. As you reach you spy a common garter snake coiled beside the cooler. Your heart leaps into your throat and you jump back with a start. Then reason and thirst prevail and you ignore the harmless snake and reach for your cold drink. But why the moment of fear? There is nothing sudden or intense or novel about a little garter snake, but it is one of the special class of dangers to which man responds with fear—probably a God-given reaction that serves us well outside the more tame environment in which most of us live. Most folks in the past and many in some parts of the world today live in the presence of wild animals, poisonous snakes, and other dangers for which it's healthy to have an automatic response of fear. But it is a small fear that a modern suburbanite can wash away with a cold drink and return again to a summertime nap.

You wake for the last time to gaze into the familiar face of the neighbor from the other side of your lot, and you read on his usually friendly countenance a scowl of anger. You recognize his expression and his rigid stance as threatening, and a sensation of fear rises within you. This time the emotion is triggered by a message communicated by a standardized expression and posture that is well understood in social interactions among human beings. It doesn't take long to handle the crisis—it was the other neighbor's new Irish elk hound, not your kids, that dug up this man's garden. Fear subsides, the friendship is maintained, but the afternoon is pretty much a total loss. You fold up your lounge and slink back into the house.

While you've probably never experienced all this fear in the course of one afternoon nap, it is likely that on different occasions you have experienced each of the four causes of fear described above: any intense stimulus like sudden pain, loud noise, or very bright light; novel or unfamiliar objects or situations; a class of natural dangers which includes snakes, large predatory animals, darkness, and very confined or very open spaces; and threatening behavior by our fellow man. It makes sense that we be prepared to deal with the dangers that could accompany loud noise or bright light or unfamiliar situations. The fear of snakes and other dangerous animals, which seems to be innate in man, is one of a class of fears which seem more important in less civilized circumstances than in countries like the United States today. Preindustrial man, particularly, probably encountered more risks in the dark than in daylight and was more vulnerable to predators in very confined spaces, where he might be trapped, or in wide open spaces, where there might be no place to hide. Finally, sad to say, we often have good cause to fear our fellow man. The communication of anger or threats plays a useful part in our social interactions. When someone threatens us, we respond with fear.

We will probably recognize that some problem fears are simply a continued operation of the basic natural fear response under circumstances where it is no longer appropriate. Excessive fear of animals, the dark, and confined or wide open spaces are examples. Most people have little reason to fear these things today, yet some continue to do so. With a little imagination we can see some likely ways that these basic fear triggers can operate in social situations. A sudden or unexpected meeting with a stranger or confrontation with an adversary might trigger fear, while a scheduled meeting or gradual approach would not. Some social situations have the characteristics of an "intense stimulus." Most people find it easier to deal with old friends than with people newly met; and with people of similar cultural background than with people who behave in very different ways. It is normal to feel more at ease at home or in the environments that we are most familiar with than in new and strange places. The experiences of life can shape these patterns in many different ways. The emotion of fear is working right for us when real dangers, not imagined ones, trigger it, and when we respond to fear in the right way.

Many of our fears are not learned, but are simply part of us. Newborn babies are afraid of loud noises, of pain, and of the sensation of falling. They don't have to be taught these fears. They are born with them fully developed. Other unlearned fears develop as a human being grows older. Babies usually develop a fear of strangers at about the age of six months. They begin to be afraid of the dark around two years of age, and their fear increases to about the age of six. Most children show no fear of snakes before two years of age, then develop a growing caution which reaches a level of full-blown fear at about four years and continues to increase after that for some additional years. Children's fear of animals increases from very early in life to about the age of two to four, then tends to decline. All these fears develop in children without any exposure to the objects themselves, let alone without having been threatened or harmed by them.

On the other hand, a very large number of our fears are learned. We are taught by parents, friends, and experience that certain objects and situations are dangerous and hence should be feared. While it's normal for a child's innate fear of animals to fade after the age of four, the little boy who is bitten by a neighbor's dog at the age of five is likely to learn to fear dogs. The more often he is bitten, the more intense and consistent the fear reaction is likely to be. Mothers and fathers teach their children not to poke screwdrivers into electrical sockets by using verbal warnings and scoldings and perhaps physical punishment. A healthy fear is taught by associating the forbidden action with unpleasant correction or punishment, rather than with the still more unpleasant and dangerous experience of electrical shock. We might learn to be afraid of water by a near-drowning experience, or of cars by being involved in a traffic accident. We might learn to fear people bigger than us or people armed with weapons by being abused, threatened, or exploited by them.

Our fear reactions change as our lives unfold. Some of our fears fade away with age, while new ones grow up in their place. This may happen in an orderly and useful way, or it may be the source of disorder in our lives. Some people, for example, carry infantile fears within them throughout their lives. In other cases, we learn with age to handle or even ignore much of what we feared when young.

When I was about four or five years old the neighbor's dog bit me in the leg. I was a skinny kid so he didn't get much meat, but it did leave me a little afraid of dogs. Despite that early fear, I always liked dogs and my family always had several around. I hunted with them, handled them as pets, and as the years went by that early fear pretty much faded away. Today I have a whole yard full of dogs—my neighbors probably wish

I'd never overcome my fear. One day I had to rescue a good boat from the jaws of my biggest dog to prevent him from chewing it up. I grabbed his upper and lower jaws and pried them apart by pressing the skin of his lips against his teeth—the standard method for removing an object from the mouth of a strong-jawed dog. In the middle of the operation a thought passed through my mind: "He might not like this." I felt a twinge of fear—maybe a little hangover from the fear that was planted in me when that little dog bit me when I was four or five. It wasn't a problem, though, just a passing twinge, and I was able to go ahead and do what had to be done.

I have also outgrown or at least learned to handle different kinds of social fears. I've always been a little on the shy side—shyness is a form of social fear—but I was taught at home that you had to do what was right regardless of how you felt about it. So on many occasions I grit my teeth and met strangers I didn't want to meet and attended parties and ceremonies and other social events that made me uncomfortable because I dislike swirling crowds of people. When I first began attending the university, my father told me that I should show a selection of my closeup photographs of wildflowers and insects to the professor who was head of the natural history program which I wanted to enter. The thought of doing anything so brash horrified me. But one day I took my pictures to the professor's office; as my bad luck would have it, he was in. I trooped passed his door four or five times; sauntered up and down the halls trying to look casual; drank out of every water fountain in the building; visited the men's room two or three times—and the professor was still in. My fear of visiting him—which I preferred to think of us as a becoming reserve—was surpassed only by my fear of my father. I overcame my shyness, knocked on his door, was courteously received, showed him my pictures, and eventually spent two very profitable summers at the biological field station he directed.

I vividly remember that experience of confronting and walking through a fear. That one experience didn't cure me completely, and I've had to repeatedly confront shyness hundreds of times over the years. But it was certainly the hardest experience of the kind, and all the others have been easier since. I should confess that I still experience some shyness and haven't gained as much ground in that area of my life as I did with the dog-bite fear. But I have come a long way, and for the most part I'm able to act responsibly in the different life situations that I have to deal with.

Just as we need to overcome some fears as we grow older, we need to acquire others. I grew up in a small town where people often walked in the woods and on the streets at night. Many years later during periodic business trips to a large city, it was my practice to take long walks in the evenings for exercise. I assumed, without thinking, that if it was safe to walk in the woods or on the streets of a small town at night, it was safe to do so anywhere.

When my business clients learned of my exercise habit, they were horrified and immediately took pains to teach me that I was in great danger in walking the city streets at night. I had to be taught a fear that was useful. And when they told me about the things that happened in their city at night, I had no difficulty at all in being afraid.

However, part of growing into maturity is learning to manage acquired fears. For example, we may have acquired a reasonable fear of tobogganing by hearing stories of friends' injuries or experiencing the sensation of losing control at high speed. But a little careful and disciplined practice might well teach us that tobogganing is enjoyable, and that the risk can be reduced to an acceptable level. With experience we overcome or learn to manage the fear of strangers, of the dark, of some loud noises, or unfamiliar places. To become a healthy, well-balanced human being, we should find ourselves growing out of old, useless fears and into useful new fears as time goes on.

The same is true for social fears and anxious concerns. As we grow toward adulthood we should experience growing confidence in ourselves, in our ability to relate and to serve others, and in others' willingness to accept us. Our fear of meeting new people or of making mistakes should lessen. Likewise, we should learn to deal effectively with the concerns in life that we can handle and not to be overcome by those that we are powerless to change. All this should, in a sense, happen in the natural course of events. Often it does not because of our inner weaknesses and because we may experience real mistreatment and rejection by others. We may also find our lives or the lives of our loved ones marred by serious difficulties. But the bad experiences of life do not have free reign in shaping the way our emotions work in social situations or in dealing with concrete dangers. The power of God is at work to overcome the effects of evil in the lives of his sons and daughters.

This description of what fear is, how it develops in our lives, and how it can work for both good and bad should help to dispel much of the mystery about it. Understanding fear doesn't give us the power to overcome problem fears by our own unaided efforts. It does enable us, however, to cooperate with God as he works to change problem patterns in our lives. The Lord might choose to miraculously and instantaneously free us from problem fears, but it is much more likely that he will choose to work with nature. As he releases his power through channels of wisdom, discipline, training, and the development of sound relationships, he will bring us freedom from fear.

So far I have discussed only the natural sources and causes of fear. As Christians we know that reality extends far beyond that which can be seen and felt and measured, to include spiritual beings and forces which profoundly affect our lives. We face natural dangers of a random or nonpurposeful kind, but we also face spiritual dangers which are purposeful and devious—a part of the spiritual warfare in which all Christians are involved. Few of us are ever in a situation where we need to fear being hunted down and eaten by a wolf or a lion; yet all of us are warned, "Your adversary the devil prowls around like a roaring lion, seeking someone to devour" (1 Pt 5:8).

We are stalked, attacked, preyed upon by Satan and evil spirits, and one of the major weapons they use against the Christian is fear. This often happens through the work of an evil spirit reinforcing a basic natural fear. For example, some people, instead of outgrowing or learning to constructively manage fear of the dark, find this fear growing into a major cause of bondage in their lives. The reason can be the work of an evil spirit stirring up emotions and implanting irrational thoughts in their minds. Sometimes the Evil One mounts a massive spiritual assault by attempting to grip the Christian with a nameless, faceless fear that chokes his spirit and seems to extend its tentacles into every area of his life. More subtly, the Evil One often teaches fear by stirring up unpleasant thoughts or emotions whenever we seek to act in some especially righteous way—with great generosity or patience or faith. The connection between a righteous desire and an unpleasant thought or feeling makes us reluctant (a subtle fear) to act righteously. To whatever natural fearful tendencies we have the Devil adds plain, old-fashioned temptation—a spiritual push toward the darkness of fear. Just as God works through both the natural and the spiritual orders to form us and bless us, Satan works through them to attack us, seeking to destroy us. Spiritual workings of fear, such as described here, are not just small effects added to our natural fears, but powerful forces of evil which hold many people in deep bondage.

Fear of things spiritual is another class of problems which can be especially severe for some Christians. We usually and quite properly think of spiritual forces as beyond our control. If things natural are to be feared, then things spiritual are to be feared even more. Some people are terrified of Satan and of alien spiritual powers, both real and imagined. They do not know how to stand on the spiritual authority over evil that is the heritage of every Christian. A healthy fear of evil spiritual forces is wise; helpless terror in the face of evil is bondage.

Some people feel guilty about sins they have committed and are afraid that they will go to hell when they die. They either don't understand God's call to repentance and offer of forgiveness, or else they don't really trust in God's promises—that is, they have a problem of faith. Others fear damnation based on a general feeling of unworthiness rather than on any specific wrongdoing in their lives. They know about God's promise of forgiveness of sin and salvation and believe it to a certain degree in their minds, but are still plagued by emotions of fear. Sometimes the truths that we understand in our minds don't easily become spiritual realities, matters of conviction of heart.

We have to wage a struggle against our own weaknesses and against those spiritual forces that oppose God's work in our lives.

Another kind of fear problem in the spiritual realm comes not from wrong attitudes about ourselves, but from wrong attitudes about God. Some folks think of God as indifferent, cold, or vindictive. They know of God, but they don't really know him personally. They experience spiritual loneliness and isolation because they wrongly imagine that God is unapproachable or unconcerned about them.

If you think about it, all of these fears in the spiritual realm are counterparts to familiar patterns in human relationships—only worse. If the possibility of displeasing or offending your friends and neighbors makes you feel afraid, the possibility of offending or displeasing God will make you more afraid. If it hurts a little bit to think that other people don't like you, it will hurt a lot if you think that God doesn't like you. If you are afraid of people who might withhold affection, damage your reputation, harm you physically, or even kill you, how much more would you be afraid of God who has the power to cast you into hell for all eternity. But if fear is greater in the spiritual realm, the power that frees us from fear is also greater. This power is the very power of God. Repentance, forgiveness, healing, deliverance, divine wisdom, faith—all these are given to us that we might become truly free men and women in Jesus Christ.

THREE

Fear—Good or Bad?

SOME PEOPLE EQUATE fear with cowardice, and so think of it as always bad. Many others experience fear as a crippling problem, a form of bondage that brings suffering throughout their lives. These people too find it difficult to see any fear as being good. Yet this view is mistaken. Fear is a God-given emotion. Fear in itself is basically good so long as it works in right order in our lives. Fear is working in good order if we experience it at the right times and if it leads us to do the right things. If we experience fear when no danger is present, then it is bad for us. If it causes us to act wrongly—for example, to run away when we should stand and fight—then it is also bad. If a fear, useful as a momentary experience, lives on to become a constant, nagging internal state, then it has become a problem. In short, fear can be good or bad, depending on circumstances.

Some specific kinds of fear, however, are basically good in themselves, while others are basically bad. Fear of God and reverence for him or for his name are always good. Having respect for laws and for those in authority who administer them is a good fear. These fears become bad only if we apply them to some wrong object—for example, if we were to revere Satan or have respect for criminals.

Fear as an emotional reaction to real physical danger is good because it prepares us to handle the situation by fighting or fleeing. If, while crossing a highway on foot, you see a trailer truck barrelling down on you, the fear you experience should lead you to run away. This instant emotional reaction might save your life, where pausing to think about the danger might take so much time that you would be killed before you decided to get out of the way. Fear can also cause us to fight a danger. If the grass in the vacant lot behind your house catches fire, the fear you feel as you see the flames licking skyward and advancing toward your house is probably a warning to stand and fight the fire, rather than to run away and leave your place to be burned. We teach our children not to poke screwdrivers in wall sockets or put their hands on hot stove burners, and to handle cars and knives safely. What we instill in them is not bondage to unreasonable fear but a healthy fear that protects them from harm. In fact, in most instances this kind of training enables people to avoid these dangers so that they won't have to confront them imminently, or suffer physical harm, or experience the emotion of fear as an emergency reaction.

Fear that causes us to choose our words carefully in a personal relationship or social situation in order to avoid being misunderstood (this kind of fear would be called "caution") would ordinarily be a good fear so long as it was not based on self-concern and did not inhibit us in relating to other people.

Sometimes a good fear can go bad. One of the most common ways that this happens is to have normal, healthy fear reactions of the moment become internal dispositions or character traits. Fear is no longer useful when the danger has passed, yet we often hear people say, "I was a nervous wreck for months afterwards." I know a woman who was involved in a minor automobile accident and was afraid to drive a car for years afterwards. I could understand that it would take her a few days or even a few weeks to get over the experience of fear caused by the accident. But the fear that continued to grip her over a period of years was an irrational one. It wasn't preventing her from taking unreasonable risks; it was simply depriving her of the convenience of being able to drive. She was becoming a "fearful" person.

I went to high school with a boy who was called on without warning to make an informal speech in English class. He wasn't a particularly confident guy and the sudden challenge scared him out of his wits. Actually, he did well at giving the speech, considering the state he was in. But no amount of assurance or consolation by his friends could convince him of this. From that point on, he lived in constant fear of being called upon for another speech and could hardly stand to go to English class. Eventually he was called upon to make another presentation, again without warning. His second experience was worse than his first because now the justifiable "fear of the moment" was compounded by the internal fear disposition that he had so carefully nourished.

Fears which have become character traits, parts of our personal makeup which shape our dispositions or emotional states, are the most troublesome fears most of us face. I call them "chronic internal" fears.

Social fears in particular tend to take this form. Some chronic internal fears fix on personal relationships (i.e., they are social fears), while others fix on concrete external dangers (usually ones that are vague or distant or hard to do anything about). Since chronic internal fears are so common today, it is worth spending some time discussing them in more detail, seeing where they come from and how they work.

The first thing to say is that the commonness of this kind of fear today is ironic. We live in a world with many fewer objective dangers than people in past societies faced. Ninety percent of all the human beings who have ever lived were primitive hunter-gatherers. They spent most of their time in a single pursuit—trying to scrounge enough food to survive. Another six percent were primitive farmers. Their life was quite a bit safer than the hunter-gatherer's, but primitive farmers still faced much more real danger than most of us do. We are numbered among the small percentage of people who have enjoyed the advantages of industrial society. Infant and childhood diseases have been drastically reduced. Few large animals roam around eating people. A more organized society offers protection from bandits and local tribal warfare. In the developed nations, supplies of water, fuel, and shelter are reasonably stable and adequate. A newborn baby girl in ancient Rome had a life expectancy of twenty-one years. A baby girl born in the United States today has a life expectancy of nearly seventy-five years.

Despite crime, social unrest, wars, rumors of wars, occasional localized famines and outbreaks of disease, the increase in life expectancy throughout the world is clear evidence that the number of dangers people face today has declined greatly. But new dangers of unprecedented kinds replace the old ones. We have developed modern methods of nuclear, chemical, and biological warfare which could quickly envelop whole continents or even the entire globe; the individual has little defense against them. The "new" dangers are impersonal and untouchable; they hang over our lives like a dark cloud.

The second change has been the development of modern communications, which blesses us with the latest bad news from every corner of the globe. We quickly hear about the tidal wave in Australia, the train wreck in Pakistan, the terrorist assasination in Italy, the race riot in an American city, and the new pollutant oozing out of our water tap. Some of the bad news is directly threatening to us. But most of it simply keeps us informed of misfortunes that have come upon others in far-away places—misfortunes which stir our concern but which we can do little about.

A third type of change has affected social patterns to bring fear into human relationships. Many forms of stable traditional social relationships are breaking down in the face of change brought about by modern technology. Families experience isolation from one another and alienation within. People uproot themselves and move away in search of jobs or sunshine. God-given basics for solid personal relationships are lost. People's minds are gripped by self-concern. Perhaps we have more causes than ever before for chronic internal fears and anxieties, particularly those relating to human relationships. Perhaps this is why the sum total of fear in human life seems to be greater today than at any time in human history.

To a certain degree, fear of loneliness, failure, and rejection in our society is justified. If you don't conform to majority values you are likely to end up a lonely outcast. If you fail to produce according to the demands of the economic system, your employer is likely to discard you. Sometimes people are rejected for real faults, sometimes for trivial imperfections, sometimes even for virtues. Christians should be better able to deal with such fears, because of trust in God, personal righteousness, good supportive relationships, stable families and communities. But many Christians fail to live according to God's wisdom for life and so deprive themselves of the protection from fear that is rightfully theirs.

Chronic internal fear can be triggered by a traumatic experience. The pain of betrayal in a trusted personal relationship or the sudden death of a loved one or a severe financial loss—such experiences can often lead to a chronic state of anxiety or pessimism. Living with possible but unconfirmed danger can also lead to chronic fear. If we decide that danger does not exist or that we can accept the risk, fear should fade. Some people, however, leave the issue undecided and sink into prolonged fretting, anxiety, and fearfulness. Many are like a woman I know who is sensitive to every arching of the eyebrows, every subtle inflection or tone of voice in conversations with friends and acquaintances. "What did she mean by that?" "Did I do something to offend her? She gave me such a funny look." Such people leave themselves stewing with these kinds of questions—afraid that their friends are rejecting them—yet never airing their concerns and clearing up possible misunderstandings. They live in constant anxiety that their most trusted relationships are deteriorating; that others don't respect or love them; that they are unintentionally doing things wrong.

Another common example is the person who goes to extremes in grooming and dress because of fear of rejection by other people. In college I knew of some girls who spent hours each morning in front of the mirror desperately trying to improve the face that God had given them and spent hundreds of dollars on clothes in the latest styles from the finest shops—all because they were afraid they might otherwise fail to win acceptance in the crowd they went with.

Chronic internal fears such as the ones we have been discussing are commonly expressed in habits such as caution or conservativism, timidity or cowardice. It is possible to identify a whole constellation of related fears which operate as traits of character or dispositions or habits in our lives. We speak of various people as being cowardly, timid, cautious, hesitant, anxious, lacking in self-confidence, conservative, insecure, retiring, reserved, or inhibited. The meaning of these terms in common use and the fears themselves tend to overlap somewhat. But they are meaningful terms, helpful to our discussion.

From the constellation of overlapping fears listed above, we will take a closer look at six very common ones: caution, conservatism, cowardice, timidity, insecurity, and anxiety. Caution and conservatism can often serve a good purpose, but they become unhealthy traits if they direct our approach to all situations in life. Cowardice, timidity, insecurity, and anxiety, on the other hand, are always bad forms of fear because they lead us to act in wrong ways or burden us with unnecessary suffering.

First, consider caution. Caution is working right when it leads us to think prudently in advance so we can minimize the risks we take. Overly cautious people, however, are fearful people. They always check things out very carefully and don't act until they are absolutely certain that the situation is safe. A cautious person might take the time to shake out the sheets and blankets before crawling into bed each night in case snakes might have crawled in among the bedding. This makes good sense if you are camping out in a swamp in Georgia. It makes no sense in a modern home with a tight foundation, windows, and doors. I know many men who have refused more challenging and rewarding jobs because they were afraid they might fail. Some of them could have made it much bigger in their careers, but they were simply too cautious to enter a situation where they had to run any significant risk of failure. These men never balanced the possibility of failure against the benefits of a more challenging and rewarding job.

I grew up with kids whose mothers wouldn't let them go outside to play if there was dew on the grass. "You might get your feet wet and catch a bad cold," the mothers said. Millions of kids have played in wet grass and never caught colds; at any rate, colds are seldom fatal. The danger of being formed in a fearful personality is far greater than the danger of getting wet feet and a head cold.

One common form of caution is unique to certain Christians. These are people who are reluctant to surrender their lives more fully to the Lord because they are uncertain about what changes he may want to make. Caution in avoiding the "unknown" plays a stronger role in their lives than their trust in God, even when they genuinely desire to enter into a deeper relationship with him.

These wrong kinds of caution cost more than time and wasted effort; they clutter the mind, misshape the personality, and rob people of life's greatest rewards.

Some cautions are sensible, however. If you must walk through a patch of poison ivy, do it with great caution. Don't spread your picnic blanket on a red ant hill. Ask for references before you hire household help. Check out the company before you invest your life's savings in stock. Take along a raincoat if you visit Seattle in November. Don't seek advice from strangers. By all means, don't take a job for which you are obviously unqualified. These are all sensible cautions. But an overly cautious personality—one which is always fearful and preoccupied with security, which refuses to take risks because of possible or imagined dangers—can shrivel your life. You take walks in the park only with the greatest hesitancy and care because you are afraid you might step on something—a sharp stick, a hole, pigeon droppings, a fragile flower. Maybe you avoid picnics because there may be ants, or you are afraid to get help in your household even when you desperately need it. Perhaps you avoid advice even from friends, or sew your life savings up in a mattress where they are quickly eaten up by the inflation moth. Do you take a raincoat along when you visit Phoenix in

September? These are all signs of an overly cautious personality, a personality shaped by fear. You will miss a lot of the fun in life, pass up many opportunities to learn, to secure help, or even to make money. You pay an unreasonably high price for insurance against dangers that probably don't exist, or could be readily overcome if they did. You trudge through life bearing an unnecessary burden of concern, a burden that takes up time and energy, that takes up room in your thought life, and that weighs down your spirit.

Conservatism is an inclination to avoid change or things new and different and to cling to existing ideas, institutions, and ways of behaving. Like caution it can be either good or bad. There's something to be said for sticking to the old tried and tested approaches to life. In preindustrial society, the margin for survival was too narrow to allow much experimentation. When you are barely making it under the best of circumstances you can't afford many mistakes. If taste-testing a new wild plant results in your hallucinating when it's time to bring in the wheat crop, you and your family may starve in the coming winter. If the spearhead you attached by that clever new method comes loose when you're attacking a hungry panther, you may not even make it *into* the coming winter.

In modern times, we can see about us tremendous changes in the way that human society operates—both good and necessary changes which adapt us to modern technological life, and bad and unnecessary changes which have drawn man out of the pattern for successful human life that God himself ordained. Modern medical technology provides effective cures for many diseases which formerly were usually fatal. This same medical technology provides the option of cheap and readily available abortion, through which millions of human lives are taken. Modern transportation systems distribute foodstuffs quickly from areas of surplus to areas of need. Modern transportation also contributes to the social mobility that uproots families from familiar surroundings and relationships with relatives and friends, and transplants them into new and less stable social settings. We should welcome the good changes that modern advances have brought. But a healthy dose of conservative suspicion of many of these new patterns is a useful instinct for the modern Christian, particularly suspicion of changes that weaken family life and erode Christian morality.

Conservatism has a definite place in life when change exposes us to great dangers or to the loss of something that is an important good. It would be fair to say that Christianity itself is inherently conservative in that it is founded upon God's eternal, unchanging truth. However, an overdose of conservatism—approaching everything with a reluctance to welcome change—causes this character trait to take the form of a problem fear.

Take evangelism, for example. Jesus commanded that his disciples preach the gospel to all nations, even to the end of the earth. This commission is passed on to us Christians today. Now Jesus and the first disciples did their preaching without the aid of any electronic amplifiers or loudspeaker systems, and without radio, television, or even a printing press. In the early days of Christianity, they picked a spot on a hillside where they might get a good echo and preached there. An overly conservative Christian today might insist that since Jesus didn't use a loudspeaker or the radio, we too should limit ourselves to spreading the gospel by unaided word of mouth. But it would seem foolish indeed to forgo all the modern means for spreading the gospel truth at our disposal. It might even be argued that today for the first time, with all the electronic media at our disposal, it is at last possible to truly preach the gospel to the ends of the earth.

Life changes rapidly in today's world, and if we don't adapt by inventing new approaches we may not be able to keep up with the times. What worked last year may be useless for this year's problems. In the past it was customary to trade or pay cash for nearly everything that was acquired. Who today would think of paying the total price in cash when buying a new home or a farm? Most of us would never be able to afford one if we insisted on paying in full at the time of purchase. Even if we could afford it, paying in full at the outset might be a serious economic mistake in the complicated society that we live in.

Nevertheless, many people cling to the old and

familiar, not because the old things are necessarily good or better in themselves, but because these people fear change. The chronically conservative person doesn't make new friends, doesn't take a better job when he can, isn't particularly open to growing in character, to getting free of faults. He or she might not like the new and different self. Like caution, conservativism working in the wrong way can cripple your personality and make life a sad, stunted affair.

In contrast to caution and conservatism, which can be either useful traits or problems, cowardice is always bad. When confronted by real danger and the fear that it arouses, we should often stand and fight rather than run away. If you flee when you should stand, you're a coward. Cowardice is not the same thing as being afraid. It is doing the wrong thing in response to fear.

A boy who learns in early life to fear the normal rough and tumble play of childhood should overcome this fear. He might confront it on reasonably safe grounds by joining a soccer team. Yet if he surrenders to the fear and takes up stamp collecting instead, he may be a coward.

If a little girl who can't swim falls in the river near you, and you have a chance to save her, it would be cowardly not to jump in and attempt the rescue. Even if you must take a considerable risk, you should give it a try. If you stand on the bank and rationalize, "We might both drown," or, "Somebody farther downstream will probably get her," or, "Maybe she'll learn to swim real quick," you're a coward.

If a powerful and ruthless man who is respected by many people spreads lies which damage the reputation of one of your friends, you should come to your friend's defense. Maybe you are mild-mannered by nature and the thought of openly opposing this man stirs intense fear within you. He could harm you too. Standing silently aside is the most appealing option. Yet not only does loyalty demand that you defend your friend, but the aggressor represents an evil that should be opposed. It may be difficult to figure out how best to defend your friend, but the right response is to push past your fears and fight the evil at hand. Your fears, after all, have done their job of warning you of danger and preparing you to cope with it. Not to overcome these fears and act would be cowardice.

Timidity is another character trait based in fear which is always bad. It is somewhat like caution, but caution has more to do with anticipation of danger and minimizing the risk. A timid person is constantly fearful, approaches life warily, as though real danger were present at every turn, holds back in work, recreation, personal relationships, and everything else he or she does. Timidity is something like chronic low-level cowardice. It is a very common form of fear operating in personal relationships, where it is often called "shyness."

Shy people usually don't talk very much, are not

very open to others, don't mingle readily or seek people out, are hesitant in committing themselves, and are passive in personal relationships. It is difficult for others to get to know shy people. They usually don't say what they feel or think or stand for. They are afraid of doing the wrong thing or of being held in judgment or scorn. Often shy people do not act in normal natural ways: they don't speak with normal volume, they won't take a full swing at a tennis ball, and can't bring themselves to ask for seconds when their favorite dessert is on the dinner table. Shyness not only cuts people off from the support of others that they desperately need, but it deprives them of the opportunity to use their own gifts in service of others. They are hesitant to greet people, show them hospitality, ask what their needs are. Often they are inhibited in joining in group activities like singing, dancing, or working together. Sometimes shyness is mistaken for a virtue. "She's such a nice, quiet girl," people will say. But there is a world of difference between someone with a genuine quiet spirit and someone who is in bondage to fear.

The timid or shy person is cowed by fear (conscious or unconscious) that they "can't do it," or will be disliked or rejected if they try to "do it," or that "maybe they shouldn't do it," and that somehow, in some way, they are in danger of getting hurt. Like the case of unhealthy caution, timid people miss many of the pleasures, opportunities to serve, chances to advance, and challenges that could help them grow in strength of character. Meekness and proper reserve place worthwhile limits on the way we behave and relate; they are virtues. Timidity places unreasonable limits on how we behave and relate; the timid person is a slave to a particular form of fear.

Insecurity is the fear that the things we depend on for safety and success may fail us or (in the social case) that others won't accept us, care for us, or accord us the position we desire. Insecure people feel that they are not firmly moored in their personal relationships and jobs. Things might break loose and leave them adrift. They usually feel an overwhelming need for reassurance and affirmation, and place an improperly high value on social acceptance. Insecurity leads people to put their trust in others or in the things of the world, rather than in the Lord, and to base their sense of self-worth on others' response to them. Very often, insecure people will hide their weakness under a facade of bluster and pretence. Sometimes they succeed in fooling many people, with the result that their friends treat them as confident, well-balanced individuals, and leave them to deal with their internal misery alone. More often, however, the fear shows through despite their best efforts to cover up.

You are putting up a facade if you are afraid to relate to other people according to the way you truly are. Despite your insecurity, you may talk confidently, even aggressively or boastfully, because you think that an exaggerated display of virtues and accomplishments will win others' acceptance. You may even take on special mannerisms, conversational style, tastes and values in order to gain acceptance. You may express pleasure and approval of others which you don't really feel, in order to win their friendship. The tragedy is that this way of dealing with fear leaves the real problem untouched, as well as partly hidden away where it is harder than ever to deal with.

Anxiety is another very common form of internal fear. Anxiety is chronic uneasiness of mind over some anticipated misfortune. Anxious people are usually unsure whether the misfortune is real. Sometimes anxiety fixes on a particular subject like money; sometimes it is a general state of worry with no particular focus. Anxious people feel like fish out of water. Things go bad for them. They look for the next hardship or disaster. Life is one continuing dull, fearful worry. They doubt their ability to cope with the misfortune when it arrives. Anxiety is sometimes a gnawing background fear, but it can become an overwhelming and paralyzing form of bondage. It is proper to take a constructive concern for the challenges of life, but to worry all the time with no particular reason and no solution in sight is to suffer from the form of fear called anxiety.

A key characteristic of anxiety is its vagueness, uncertainty, and generality. The sufferer often loses a clear sense of the source of the problem. Some anxiety-ridden people may know what they are anxious about, but not know exactly why. For example, I know people but have plenty of money but still feel anxious about their finances. The question "Why are you anxious?" has no clear answer. Almost anything can contribute to a state of anxiety. A person may fear his own death or the possible death of loved ones, the loss of his possessions, sickness, or loss of favor with God. Chronic guilt can be a form of spiritual anxiety. One of the most common causes of anxiety is disorder in personal relationships. People are anxious over the prospect of not succeeding, of being disliked, of making mistakes, and of inadvertently hurting others.

It is important to understand the difference between anxiety and taking a constructive concern for a problem. "Concern" often leads to effective action. You either change things to eliminate the cause of fear or you determine that there is nothing you can do and therefore decide to put aside the concern. Anxiety, on the other hand, is a continuous stewing over real or imagined dangers without any effective attempt to deal with the source of the fear, analyze the problem, get help, or change things in life.

The tragedy of chronic internal fears, especially social ones, is compounded in that they often cause an increase in the very thing we are afraid of. Fear is sometimes caused by loneliness, failure, and rejection, but fear often causes these things as well. Fear is a prison that isolates men and women from others. Fear is a prison that multiplies fear.

These are some of the ways in which fear, a basically good emotion, can work against us.

Unpleasant stuff to consider, but in no way a cause for discouragement. As we grow in the Christian life, we should cast off and outdistance these fears one by one. We should grow in character so that useless fears have no place in our life, and good, God-given fears lead us to act righteously.

FOUR

Marks of the Christian: Confidence, Boldness, and Courage

WHEN NO REAL DANGER threatens, the Christian man or woman with well-formed character should experience no fear. When danger threatens, normal wholesome fear should sound an alert and trigger preparations of body, mind, and spirit to deal with the situation. You may read this and be tempted to complain that "that all sounds so neat and simple, but it isn't the way that it happens with me. Why don't I work that way?" The answer might be that you haven't yet fully tapped into the spiritual resources that enable you to deal with fear. These are resources available to every Christian, and among them is a personal character formed in the image and likeness of your heavenly Father. None of us has our character yet formed perfectly in this image, but some are much farther along the road than others. To understand the kind of people that God intends us to be, we need only turn to the teaching of scripture. There we will discover that Christians should be able to approach life with certain God-given character traits that reinforce our freedom from fear in situations that are neutral and enable us to respond correctly when we experience fear as a result of real danger.

The first of these marks or character traits in the Christian is confidence. Even in the face of great danger, the Christian should be confident. In Proverbs 3:25 we are told, "Do not be afraid of sudden panic, or of the ruin of the wicked when it comes; for the Lord will be your confidence and will keep your foot from being caught." Confidence, like all other God-given traits, is founded in the Lord himself and not in human strength or in clever psychological ploys which insulate us from fear. More specifically, we are told in Proverbs 14:26 that "in the fear of the Lord, one has strong confidence, and his children will have a refuge." I will say more later about "fear of the Lord," which turns out to be the grandest of the good fears and one of the principal weapons for dealing with problem fears.

We might think of confidence as a consciousness of our ability to succeed, a freedom from uncertainty or embarrassment. Because we trust in God's promises, we are sure that things in life will ultimately work out, no matter how uncertain they seem now. "He has said, 'I will never fail you nor forsake you.' Hence we can confidently say, 'The Lord is my helper. I will not be afraid. What can man do to me?'" (Heb 13:5-6) Because of our trust in God's power at work in our lives, we are conscious of our ability to relate to other people in a loving way, and confident too of their capacity to respond well to us. As Christians we are not making a hollow boast when we say, "I can do all things in him who strengthens me" (Phil 4:13).

If a child in our care got lost on a dark and stormy night, we could readily risk danger to ourselves in searching for it, confident of the Lord's care for us. The Lord may protect us from harm, perhaps in some miraculous way. But even if we stumbled into a sinkhole in the dark and drowned or were crushed by a falling tree, we could still be confident in the Lord's ultimate care and freely lay down our life to serve another. Confidence makes it possible for us to do what's right in the face of danger.

We can approach social relationships with confidence too. Often, personal relationships are completely safe, especially among Christians with whom we share a committed life. But sometimes we run the risk of being disliked, given a cold shoulder, rejected. Despite these risks the Lord wants us to act with a real confidence that we can love other people and that they ultimately will respond well to us. Because of this confidence we can be open, expressive, and decisive in our social relationships, not timid and fearful.

Boldness is a second mark of the Christian in facing situations that stir up fear. We should act with boldness, especially when we know the Lord wants us to do something. We can be daring, adventurous, properly aggressive, not inhibited or made less effective by hesitancy or reserve. Again, the character trait is rooted in our relationship with God. In this case, scripture connects it with righteous living: "The wicked flee when no one pursues, but the righteous are bold as the lion" (Prv 28:1).

Paul, writing to the Philippians from Rome after he had been imprisoned for being an apostle, describes how boldness should work. He writes:

> I want you to know, brethren, that what has happened to me has really served to advance the gospel, so that it has become known throughout the whole praetorian guard and to all the rest that my imprisonment is for Christ; and most of the brethren have been made confident in the Lord because of my imprisonment, and are much more bold to speak the word of the Lord without fear. (Phil 1:12-14)

The apparent misfortune of Paul's imprisonment, rather than frightening other Christians into hiding, as one might expect, inspired them to become more bold in speaking the word of God. Paul is obviously delighted. He points out that this is the way Christians ought to be—free to speak the word of God in spite of all risks. The Philippian Christians may have experienced natural fear of being jailed or tortured or killed, but they went ahead and did what was right anyway— they spoke the word of God boldly.

The fourth chapter of the Acts of the Apostles

describes another inspiring example of boldness. Peter and John had healed a crippled man, stirring up the wrath of the chief priests, the scribes, and the elders. They hauled Peter and John before a court and forbade them to speak or teach any more in the name of Jesus. Peter and John replied that they would not obey but must continue to preach the gospel. The authorities threatened them further and then let them go because they feared the people. Peter and John may well have been afraid at this display of official wrath, backed up by a believable threat. Yet they responded with boldness. They returned to their friends, explained what happened, and then they all turned to the Lord in prayer, ending:

> For truly in this city there were gathered together against thy holy servant Jesus, whom thou didst anoint, both Herod and Pontius Pilate, with the Gentiles and the people of Israel, to do whatever thy hand and thy plan had predestined to take place. And now, Lord, look upon their threats, and grant to thy servants to speak thy word with all boldness, while thou stretchest out thy hand to heal, and signs and wonders are performed through the name of thy holy servant Jesus. (Acts 4:27-30)

The story concludes:

> And when they had prayed, the place in which they were gathered together was shaken; and

they were all filled with the Holy Spirit and spoke the word of God with boldness. (v. 31)

The boldness of these Christians was a result of being filled with the Holy Spirit, something that came from the grace of God. The Lord intends that each of us today receive the same grace of boldness so that we too can speak and act aggressively and decisively. This is the grace that enables us to carry our identity as Christians freely and openly rather than apologetically; to speak out against evil; to love and serve others in ways that conflict with the practices of the world; to tell non-Christians about the gift of salvation in Jesus Christ. Without this grace we might limp through our fear to do the minimum acceptable job for the Lord. With the grace of boldness, we firmly and decisively plow through the opposition that fear throws up. It allows us to aggressively—even adventurously—do the full job the Lord calls us to.

Opportunities for acting with Christian boldness are by no means limited to the preaching of the gospel. The second of the two great commandments is to love our neighbor as ourselves. Unfortunately, a kind of fear called self-concern often significantly limits our ability to serve others. Even when we want to serve others, we tend to hesitantly count the cost to ourselves. Charity may pose a subtle danger to our own welfare; self-concern quickly informs us the danger is too great.

Here, as in the case of preaching the gospel, the gift of boldness stamps out hesitancy in serving others. We know the Lord wants us to love and serve others, to put their welfare ahead of our own, and by the power of the Holy Spirit we don't hesitate or hold back. Our character is formed by the gift of boldness so that we may freely, aggressively, adventurously pour ourselves out in love and service to others.

When faced by danger and the fear it stirs, a Christian should be courageous, as well as confident and bold. St. Paul exhorts in 1 Corinthians 16:13-14: "Be watchful, stand firm in your faith, be courageous, be strong. Let all that you do be done in love." Courage is a strength of mind and will that enables us to resist opposition, danger, hardship, to do what is right in spite of dangers and the fears that they arouse.

Being courageous does not mean we are free of the emotion of fear. Rather, it means being willing to act uprightly despite the fear that we have. If you discover a very large and strong robber choking your frail little grandmother to death, that overpowering sensation of fear you experience just before you tackle him doesn't mean that you're a coward. You are a coward only if you stand there apologetically, twisting your handkerchief in your hands while the murderer does his job. You are likely to find yourself in situations where you should act courageously simply because it is the right thing to do: when someone ridicules God's truth in your presence; when members of your family or those for whom you are responsible at work need correction; when you are invited to take on heavy responsibilities through which you have an opportunity to serve others or to do good; when social pressures or ridicule from friends and associates make it hard to live righteously; when you should protect the rights and reputation of others—especially the weak and the helpless. Christians may often feel fear in situations like these, but they should not allow their behavior to be ruled by it.

I learned a lesson about acting in confidence, boldness, and courage on a family camping trip in Montana. We do a fair amount of canoeing near our home in Michigan, where the rivers are mostly smooth and gentle flowing. In a few places there are short rapids which are exciting to us but wouldn't rate a second look from an experienced whitewater canoeist. Our experience is pretty much limited to these calm kinds of rivers.

On vacation in Montana, however, Paul, my youngest son, proposed that we run a quarter mile stretch of seething white water in our open canoe. We had never run white water with the speed, drop, and turbulence of this particular stretch. I couldn't guarantee that we could make it through without getting swamped. On the other hand, we knew how to handle a canoe, and running that white water looked like it would be a lot of fun. I studied that stretch of river carefully and tried to decide whether it would be irresponsible to take my youngest son and try running it. I honestly admit that the prospect scared me a bit. I knew I had an obligation to protect my son from unreasonable danger, and I tried to explain that to him. He just answered, "That's okay, Dad. I understand," in a very tolerant tone. Did my own son think I was afraid? I had to protect us from unreasonable danger. On the other hand, we knew something about handling a canoe in white water and we were good swimmers. I said to Paul, "Let's go."

We launched the canoe about fifty yards above the frothing white water in a very calm, smooth-flowing stretch. As we eased our way downstream, the roaring of the rapids grew louder and louder. The current sped up. Downstream I could see plumes of spray dashing off the larger boulders and standing waves two and three feet high. About twenty yards from the head of the rapids I asked myself how I had ever gotten into this predicament. I began to think that there was something wrong with my kid, that he lacked normal, decent fear of these kinds of dangers. I thought that if we made it through the rapids, he would just try something else equally or even more foolish and undoubtedly would never live to see the age of twenty-five. About ten yards above the head of the rapids—somewhat beyond the point of no return—Paul turned in the canoe and said to me, "Isn't this great, Dad? You feel that fear rising inside you, then you're into the white water and all you can do is paddle like mad, and the fear goes away and you just enjoy the excitement." This was much more white water than either of us had ever been in before. I remember thinking as we plunged through the first curtain of spray and bounced off the first couple of rocks, "My kid is normal—it may be the last discovery I make in this life, but my kid is normal."

We made it through. It was very exciting, and the roughest parts of the rivers back home will never be the same again to us. My son was right— without the risk it wouldn't have been nearly as much fun. After running those rapids, I knew that it had been a perfectly reasonable risk.

All the more in many situations in life it's right to push beyond the fear that warns us of danger, to take on considerable risks, in order to do what is right to serve our fellow man, to defend justice, or to resist evil. Fear only informs us of danger. It doesn't tell us whether we should accept the risk. We should examine the situation and ask whether courage would have us push on.

When Joshua was appointed to head the people of Israel, Moses gave the following exhortation to courage:

> "I am a hundred and twenty years old this day; I am no longer able to go out and come in. The Lord has said to me, 'You shall not go over this Jordan.' The Lord your God himself will go over before you; he will destroy these nations before you so that you shall dispossess them; and Joshua will go over at your head as the Lord has spoken. And the Lord will do to them as he did to Sihon and Og, the kings of the Amorites,

and to their land, when he destroyed them. And the Lord will give them over to you, and you shall do to them according to all the commandments which I have commanded you. Be strong and of good courage, do not fear or be in dread of them: for it is the Lord your God who goes with you; he will not fail you nor forsake you."

Then Moses summoned Joshua and said to him in the sight of all Israel, "Be strong and of good courage, for you shall go with this people into the land which the Lord has sworn to their fathers to give them; and you shall put them in possession of it. It is the Lord who goes before you; he will be with you, he will not fail you or forsake you; do not fear or be dismayed." (Dt 31:2-8)

A little later, the Lord spoke to Joshua, "The Lord commissioned Joshua, the son of Nun, and said, 'Be strong and of good courage; for you shall bring the children of Israel into the land which I swore to give them: I will be with you'" (Dt 31:23). Moses and the Lord were instructing Joshua about how to respond to the very real dangers that lie just ahead. He was taking the children of Israel into a situation where they could very easily be destroyed. They were about to enter the land of a people possibly stronger than they, and perhaps to face armies much bigger than theirs. The Lord's instruction to Joshua in the situation was to not give in to fear, to be assured that the Lord would not forsake him, to be courageous and do what the Lord had commanded despite the dangers he would face. It seems the Lord was saying that the key thing in the situation was not so much to win the battle as to stand fast in the face of danger and give him the chance to act on Israel's behalf. That should be the lesson for us: we can be confident, bold, and courageous because the Lord himself is acting in the dangerous situations we face.

It's important that we not confuse these traits of Christian character with counterfeit or distorted versions. Confidence, boldness, and courage are anything but mellow, laid-back virtues, yet they can and should work in our lives in an orderly, well-balanced fashion that bears good fruit. If you were to use well-chosen words about the Lord Jesus Christ in talking to your bowling club, to people at work, or to neighbors, you may bring an unbeliever to the Lord or inspire a marginal Christian to a more fervent commitment. If, on the other hand, in sharing the Good News you grab a friend by the lapels of his sport coat, back him into a corner, and breathe the words of the gospel heavily into his face, you are being obnoxious, not bold. The result will be at best no convert and at worst a punch in the nose. If without the Lord's specific leading you were to take your life's savings out of the bank, buy a plane ticket to Iran, and preach the gospel before the Iranian parliament, the outcome would probably be no converts and possibly one dead Christian. Presumption is not the same thing as confidence. Foolhardiness is not the same thing as courage. Even the most impeccable boldness cannot be counted upon to undo serious mistakes. Martyrdom is the highest Christian ideal, the greatest privilege that God could give to us. But the idea is to get martyred for our faith in Christ, not for our stupidity or obnoxiousness.

How does the Christian know when an occasion calls for confidence, boldness, or courage? The answer involves another gift of God: the gift of wisdom. Wisdom can be both a spiritual gift especially imparted to guide us in serving the Lord and a God-given natural gift of common sense. Wisdom tells us how to distinguish between true and false confidence, boldness, and courage. Wisdom tells us when and how to temper confidence, boldness, and courage with caution or conservatism. It tells us when to take a stand and when to retreat, when to speak out and when to remain silent, when to be challenging and when to be conciliatory. After all, there is something to the old saying: "He who fights and runs away lives to fight another day."

Confidence, boldness, and courage can develop to a certain degree as purely "natural" traits. Many non-Christians have them. But we talk of them here as something developed much more fully when we regard them as the marks of the Christian. They are the very character of God himself, imparted to his sons and daughters by the working of the Holy Spirit. We have them because we are formed in his image and likeness. The Lord has told us to be confident, bold, and courageous, acting in the face of danger according to the nature that he has given us. In other words, these qualities are more than what we *do*. They involve the kind of people we *are*.

Confidence, boldness, and courage come to us as we become more and more like our heavenly Father. We cannot adopt only those character traits that we prefer and ignore others. We cannot become confident, bold, and courageous without also becoming peaceful, patient, and serving. In order to lead a righteous life, we need to have everything that God has to offer: a complete and balanced character.

Why, then, is there usually such a difference between the nature we have inherited from God and the way we actually express confidence, boldness, and courage? The answers give us important clues to growing in the character of God. For one thing, sin might still be operating in us, preventing us from fully surrendering to God and inheriting Godlike character. It's also possible that these God-given character traits may not have fully displaced habits of fear in our lives. As boldness, confidence, and courage come, fear should leave. The same grace that enables us to conquer our fears gives us the very character of God. It is also true that determined practice of character traits like confidence, boldness, and courage—even before we really "have them"—helps to crowd out fear.

I have talked about Christian character in this chapter mostly in terms of gifts of the Holy Spirit. When we are open to the action of God in our lives he sovereignly confers upon us all kinds of gifts. But it is useful to think of confidence, boldness, and courage in terms of "fruits of the Holy Spirit" as well as gifts. This orients us toward the other way that God forms our character: patient living in righteousness. As time goes on and we consistently think and act in ways reflecting God's intentions for us, character traits will grow, develop, and mature, much as fine fruit is borne on a carefully cultivated tree. If we want to be fully formed in Christian character, we must be willing to pay the price: patience, suffering, and hardship; a willingness to sacrifice our own desires and preferences so that the hand of God can mold us according to his plan.

Much of the rest of this book bears directly on cooperating with God's grace in becoming confident, bold, and courageous. It is not a matter of striving for unusual or abnormal heroism or of trying to rise above the natural, authentic "way we should be." It is essentially a matter of laying claim to the character that is our rightful inheritance.

FIVE

Standing on Solid Rock

PEOPLE HANDLE FEAR in many different ways. Our responses to fear may be reasonable or unreasonable. Some of us seek out real security. Others take refuge in imagined security. One man pursued by a dangerous enemy hides in a cave with a concealed entrance and is truly safe. Another buries his head in the sand like the fabled ostrich, and feels safe because he can no longer see his enemy. It is reasonable during a disease epidemic to stay away from crowds as much as possible, never to drink water from open ditches, and to cook food thoroughly before eating it. It is unreasonable to wear gloves and a gas mask twenty-four hours a day, to fearfully stay away from all human beings, and to refuse to eat for fear the food might be contaminated. Out of fear of physical danger, some people amass wealth, fortify their homes, collect weapons, and store food. Compelled by insecurity and other social fears, some people climb to high positions, drive fancy cars, attend charm school, and become witty conversationalists. Others responding to similar social fears avoid accomplishment like the plague, drive rusty, beat-up junkers, and become surly and abrasive social misfits.

Standing behind other fears and dwarfing them all is the fear of death. Your dangerous enemy may never catch you; war may never reach your land; you may be successful and loved and secure in personal relationships; flood or famine or plague may never come; but death will surely overtake each one of us. It's natural to fear death. As an amateur Christian philosopher in a talk I heard stated with quavering emotion, "Death is the end of life." An obvious point, but still very sobering. Death is an important reality for the Christian; for those who don't believe in God, it is a problem that can't be solved. Most of our lesser fears probably contain at least a little bit of our fear of death.

How people handle the fear of death illustrates the decisive difference between the way Christians and non-Christians cope with fear. Christians and non-Christians alike take many of the same reasonable steps to handle natural fears. Both lock doors at night in cities, eat reliable food, avoid walking across busy expressways or on the edges of cliffs, and form relationships with trustworthy friends. But the Christian view of life is radically different from the world's view, and this should mean that Christians deal with fear on an entirely different basis. As Christians, we stand on the rock of God's unchanging eternal truth. It's like standing on the highest peak and looking out over the hills and valleys below. Our footing is firm; the scene doesn't change as it does when we run from one limited vantage point to another. We have a clear and undistorted view of a much greater distance. In the light of God's truth, some things that looked very important from close up are seen to be small indeed amid the sweep of the whole landscape. From where we stand we can see the history of the world and the events of our own lives with a special balance and clarity. Because they share God's vision of reality, Christians look at and live life in a very different way than non-Christians do. This extends to the way they handle problems like fear.

Our fundamental confidence in the face of danger and fear flows from our knowledge that we were created by a loving Father who cares for us. We experience this care through natural providence—all the ordinary and ongoing ways that creation and all that it contains supports us. We also experience God's care by special providence—the many ways that he intervenes especially to guide us, protect us, heal us, and show his love for us. God cares for us according to a divine plan. Our own idea of what's best for us doesn't always line up with his. In living our life in the Lord, nothing that happens, whether it seems good or hard to us, can work to our ultimate disadvantage. What we perceive as bad times may in fact be exactly that; our confidence is that the Lord will eventually deliver us from bad times. On the other hand, what we perceive as bad times may be God's way of disciplining, tempering, or purifying us.

Being confident, bold, and courageous in the way that we deal with life does not mean that the Lord never wants or allows us to experience suffering. We aren't confident and bold and courageous because nothing in life ever happens in a way that is uncomfortable or displeasing to us. Indeed, we know that the Lord doesn't intend for us to avoid all suffering. In the first letter of Peter we read:

> Now who is there to harm you if you are zealous for what is right? But even if you do suffer for righteousness' sake, you will be blessed. Have no fear of them, nor be troubled, but in your hearts reverence Christ as Lord. Always be prepared to make a defense to anyone who calls you to account for the hope that is in you, yet do it with gentleness and reverence; and keep your conscious clear, so that, when you are abused, those who revile your good behavior in Christ may be put to shame. For it is better to suffer for doing right, if that should be God's will, than for doing wrong. For Christ also died for sins once for all, the righteous for the unrighteous, that he might bring us to God, being put to death in the flesh but made alive in the spirit.
> (1 Pt 3:13-18)

When the Lord tells us not to be fearful, he's not saying our life is going to be free of all suffering. He is saying that we can be confident that he will give us the strength to deal with suffering and will eventually bring us through the suffering to victory. Furthermore, as Christians we know that greater good comes into our lives as a result of our endurance and victory over suffering than would have been the case had we lived a life of uninterrupted tranquility and ease. That is why we can face every situation with courage. Sometimes the Lord will protect us from danger and spare us all discomfort. On other occasions, the Lord allows suffering to overtake us, but offers us the opportunity to achieve ultimate victory.

Even death has no terror for us. Because we know that the gift of eternal life is ours in Jesus Christ, we can see natural death as a transition point rather than as an end. Christians should be willing, even eager, to suffer and die for the kingdom of God. If we are not called to give our lives for the Lord in martyrdom or in heroic service to our fellow man, we face eventual natural death confidently and willingly. We experience a natural fear of death which helps us to maintain our life here on earth for the period that God has ordained. But we also see beyond this natural fear to our continuing life with the Lord.

We know too that we live in the kingdom of God—a kingdom present here and now as a witness to the world. Our scale of good and bad, success and failure, often differs greatly from that of the world. Because our treasure is stored up in heaven, we fear only the loss of eternal life, not the loss of our transient life and possessions here on earth.

Our guarantee of heavenly inheritance does not

lead us to disdain or reject the created world, but to be detached from it. We are free to use the things of this world for good, to enjoy them as gifts from God, to deal with life on earth more effectively because we are citizens of the kingdom of God. Indeed, we value this earthly life because we know that God gives his people strength, the ability to love, wisdom for living, and the opportunity to be changed more and more into his image and likeness.

Because as Christians we base our lives on these and many other truths, we live and act in ways different from the citizens of the world. Where we seem to act the same, we do so for different basic reasons. Christians might raise an army or amass wealth to deal with various dangers, but we would do so on the Lord's guidance. We would not invest our energies foolishly, compelled by unreasonable fears. Christians might rise to high social positions as a result of God's providence, but would not be driven by fears of insecurity or inferiority. Our sense of worth is based upon being sons and daughters of God, and it is reinforced in loving relationships with other Christians. We trust others to respect and love us because we are brothers and sisters in Christ, not because of our cars or our worldly charm. Driving a Cadillac and performing with perfact etiquette because of feelings of inferiority would not rid you of your fears. They would still be there, running your life. And if your car was repossessed or you embarrassed yourself in polite society, they would rear up to haunt you once again. But Christians need not rely upon temporary and cosmetic remedies for fear. They meet fears with strength and wisdom drawn from God himself.

The Christian approach to life is much more fundamental than simply a unique perspective. Being a Christian means living in a personal relationship with God the Father through his Son Jesus in the power of the Holy Spirit. It is not enough to only know *about* God and his truth. We need to truly know him as a loving Father and live in him and with him. Otherwise the dangers and difficulties of life are likely to wear down our confidence and becloud our vision. God is not a distant or occasional Father. He is involved constantly and intimately in our lives in ways that we can experience much as we experience the presence and action of our natural parents. Just as a child ought to relate to its natural parents in a free and confident way, secure in a loving relationship, so too should we relate to God as our Father. Our very life springs from him.

You probably know of children who are afraid of their parents, sometimes with cause. Perhaps the father is a tyrant or the mother is cold or cruel. Such parents, despite serious faults, may do some things for their children quite well. Maybe the tyrannical father is a good provider. But the children's fears will still prevent them from experiencing trust and security in the relationship.

They are likely to be somewhat distant and wary in relation to their parents and to benefit much less from them than they should.

God is a perfect Father. He is almighty, timeless, all knowing; the creator of heaven and earth. It is right that we relate to him in overwhelming awe and reverence. But at the same time he is infinitely loving and kind. The same God whose voice thunders upon the waters, "flashes forth flames of fire," and "strips the forests bare" (Ps 29) speaks gently and quietly in our hearts. We have no reason to relate to the Lord in timidity or servile fearfulness. Even if we should be sinful and disobedient, God calls us to repent and return to him and offers us forgiveness. We should experience complete security in God's love for us. We should relate to him with the same confidence, boldness, and courage that characterize our relationships with other people.

When we speak of relating to God in overwhelming awe and reverence, we are talking about "fear of the Lord." Even though it may not seem like it, fear of the Lord is a comfortable companion of the confidence, security, and trust we have in him. Fear of the Lord means to be in awe of his power, to behold him in fear and trembling, to respect him in the way in which a son or daughter respects a loving and protective father. If you see God's awesome power directed unerringly toward good, if you fear his judgment and righteous indignation, and if you have the assurance of his love as an obedient son or daughter, then you have little reason to fear natural dangers or your fellow man or the possibility that your needs will go unmet. This is what one of Job's friends meant when he told him in the midst of his trials, "Is not the fear of God your confidence and the integrity of your ways your hope?" (Jb 4:6) On the other hand, if you do not truly fear God—if you are not in the right relationship with him—you will not experience the full measure of his protection.

Fear of God brings courage and security. Sin brings fear. In fact, fear is first mentioned in the life of the human race on the occasion of the first sin: "But the Lord God called to the man, and said to him, 'Where are you?' And he said, 'I heard the sound of thee in the garden, and I was afraid, because I was naked; and I hid myself'" (Gn 3:9-10). Adam was afraid of God because he knew he had sinned. But the account in Genesis suggests that something more than just fear of God because of sin was at work in Adam. He didn't say, "I was afraid of thee," but rather he said, "I was afraid because I was naked." It seems that sin itself also brought fear to Adam, by making him feel vulnerable and unprotected.

God, in addressing the people of Israel, specifically links freedom from fear with righteousness and bondage to fear with sinfulness:

> If you walk in my statutes and observe my commandments and do them. . . . I will give peace in the land, and you shall lie down, and none shall make you afraid; and I will remove

evil beasts from the land, and the sword will not go through your land. . . .

But if you will not harken to me, and will not do all these commandments, if you spurn my statutes, and if your soul abhors my ordinances. . . . I will set my face against you, and you shall be smitten before your enemies; those who hate you shall rule over you, and you shall flee when none pursues you. (Lv 26:3, 6, 14-15, 17)

The man who fears God is one who obeys God's commandments. Our call to obey God is expressed in its fullness in the new covenant in terms of loving God and our fellow man. In the New Testament as well as the Old, living according to God's plan is linked specifically with freedom from fear:

There is no fear in love, but perfect love casts out fear. For fear has to do with punishment, and he who fears is not perfected in love.
(1 Jn 4:18)

Loving obedience to God and loving service to our brothers and sisters has the power to "cast out fear."

Our relationship with the Lord should be based on a lively trust that he will work in our lives. It should be difficult to fear and love God and yet fail to trust him. Yet we sometimes overlook or underestimate the degree to which God's love is focused on each of us and the way in which his power is available to us.

Sometimes we find it much easier to trust the Lord when things go well than when things are difficult. We associate good things and good times in life with God's active presence and blessing, and misfortunes and difficulties with God's absence or indifference or judgment. Thus, whenever danger threatens, you may conclude that because you are afraid God is not with you.

Actually, we should in faith trust in God's presence when danger threatens most imminently. This trust allows us to handle the dangers and the fears that they stir up. Our relationship with the Lord should involve such trust that in the face of danger we respond as David did in Psalm 31:

Yea, I hear the whispering of many—
    terror on every side!—
as they scheme together against me,
    as they plot to take my life.
But I trust in thee, O Lord,
    I say, "Thou art my God."
My times are in thy hand;
    deliver me from the hand of my
        enemies and persecutors! (Ps 31:13-15)

Basic truths such as these, and a right relationship with God, are a firm foundation from which we can take practical steps to deal with major fear problems in our lives. Basic truth and our relationship with God are the solid rock on which we stand and build. Because we stand on this unshakeable foundation, we are able to love differently, to understand life differently, to deal with dangers and respond to fears differently. But these differences between Christians and the citizens of the world don't just develop automatically by "joining up." To deal with the challenges of life—including fears—in the unique way that Christianity offers, the grace God gives must be taken and used. How to do this is the subject of the following chapters.

SIX

The Shield of Faith

FOR MANY MEN AND WOMEN the truths outlined in Chapter Five—that we stand on the solid rock of God's truth and can face life with the confidence and courage of a son or daughter of God—don't make much difference. Either they have not heard these truths, or they don't really believe them, or these truths for some reason haven't come to life for them. As a result, these people deal with fear and other problems of life while standing on the shifting sands of uncertainty rather than on the solid rock of God's truth.

The key that brings these truths to life for each of us is faith. The truths of our relationship to God are treasures lying everywhere about us. By faith we pick them up and make them our own. These truths are like a cloak to protect and warm our shivering bodies. By faith we take it and put it on. The truths of the gospel are like a book filled with wisdom for dealing with problems and achieving success in life. We might hold this book in our hands but never open it and so never benefit from it. Exercising faith is like opening the book and reading the truths it contains. Faith is a powerful weapon to use against all kinds of fears in our lives—fears of real physical dangers and the social fears so common in life today. God wants you to have this gift of faith.

Where do we get faith if we don't have it? And where do we get more if we just don't have enough? Faith comes from hearing the truth about God and believing it in the depths of our hearts. Everyone hears this truth. St. Paul speaks of it: "But I ask, have they not heard? Indeed they have; for 'Their voice has gone out to all the earth, and their words to the ends of the world'" (Rom 10:18). Here St. Paul is quoting from Psalm 19, a hymn celebrating God as Creator of the universe.

> The heavens are telling the glory of God;
>   and the firmament proclaims his handiwork.
> Day to day pours forth speech,
>   and night to night declares knowledge.
> There is no speech, nor are there words;
>   their voice is not heard;
> Yet their voice goes out through all the earth,
>   and their words to the end of the world.
>   (Ps 19:1-4)

In his letter to the Romans, St. Paul affirms that man can know God: "For what can be known about God is plain to them, because God has shown it to them. Ever since the creation of the world his invisible nature, namely, his eternal power and deity, has been clearly perceived in the things that have been made" (Rom 1:19-20). When we hear the truth of God we know it to be true because God gives to each man and woman a gift of faith through which we experience certainty, clarity, and conviction. When we accept what we know to be true, we have made the gift of faith our own. Referring to the knowledge of God as contained in the gospel, Paul says, "The righteousness of God is revealed through faith for faith" (Rom 1:17). The first gift of faith which enables us to know God brings us into a life which is lived through a continual growth in faith. The revelation of God and the gift of faith are given to us in their fullness through Jesus Christ: "He who has seen me has seen the Father" (Jn 14:9); "For in him all the fullness of God was pleased to dwell, and through him to reconcile to himself all things, whether on earth or in heaven, making peace by the blood of his cross" (Col 1:19-20).

Some of you reading this book may not know God. If you don't believe in God at all or don't believe in him as a loving Father, then you literally haven't yet begun to live. Scripture says that the wickedness of men suppresses the truth of God (Rom 1:18). That wickedness is clearly at work in ideas that question or deny the reality of God as loving Father and of Jesus Christ as the Son of God and personal savior for each of us. And it is also at work in the selfish pleasures that come to possess us. But that wickedness is likely also to be at work within your heart as well, through pride and stubbornness and self-love. Listen to the testimony of creation springing forth in Psalm 19. Listen to Paul's proclamation of the gospel: "If you confess with your lips that Jesus is Lord and believe in your heart that God raised him from the dead, you will be saved" (Rom 10:9). Yes, listen to the voice that has gone out to all the earth. Turn away from wickedness and unbelief. Believe what God is telling you in your heart to be true. Believe what he is offering you the faith to accept. This simple but profound turn of heart will bring you into new life in God, a life you live by faith.

Probably most of you who read this book are Christians. For some of you, worldly ideas or pleasures may come first in life, or at least seriously compete with the place that God occupies in your heart. Others of you may be relatively free of the influence of the world but rely on yourselves rather than on the Lord for the direction of your lives. Still others may be wise enough not to rely on yourselves and you do look to the Lord, but you do not quite know how to live by faith. What every man and woman must do is to turn away from world, self, and uncertainty and actively believe and rely on God and his promises. The more we have faith in the Lord for every need in our lives, the fewer problems we will experience with fears. This applies both to coping with the normal good fears we experience, and also to problem fears that may burden us.

The best way to shape our lives according to God's intentions is to listen to his specific directions as we find them in scripture. The psalms are filled with references to the use of faith as a means of countering fear. One of the best is Psalm 23:

> The Lord is my shepherd, I shall not want;
>   he makes me lie down in green pastures.
> He leads me beside still waters;
>   he restores my soul.
> He leads me in paths of righteousness
>   for his name's sake.
> Even though I walk through the valley of the
>   shadow of death, I fear no evil;
> for thou art with me;
>   thy rod and thy staff,
>   they comfort me.
>
> Thou preparest a table before me
>   in the presence of my enemies;
> thou anointest my head with oil,
>   my cup overflows.
> Surely goodness and mercy shall follow me
>   all the days of my life;
> and I shall dwell in the house of the Lord
>   for ever.

The psalm pictures the Lord as a shepherd caring for a flock of sheep. We are under the most competent of care—the care of God himself. When we rely on him we experience no want, we have no cause to be afraid. The picture the psalmist paints vividly describes how the Lord cares for all our physical needs. We experience a sense of peace and security. That peace isn't limited to the superficial experience of life, but penetrates to the very depths of our being. The Lord will restore our soul. We can expect to experience deep inner peace in him, to be delivered from all the hurts and anguishes and anxieties and fears and discouragements that life might expose us to. We're assured that the Lord will lead us on paths of righteousness. That means that he'll show us the right thing to do in life, guide us along the right path, fulfilling the desire of our heart to be a good and holy people. With God leading us we can experience complete confidence that our lives will go well.

All this is true "even though I walk through the valley of the shadow of death." The difficulties and dangers of life cast shadows across our path, and we are forever mindful of that big shadow, the prospect of ultimate death. But under the Lord's care we need fear no evil, either now or in the future—not even death itself. We know in faith that the Lord Jesus has won an ultimate victory over death and that in him we share that victory. Death is "the last enemy to be destroyed" (1 Cor 15:26).

Psalm 23 pictures the Lord serving us at a table, banqueting in peace and security in the very presence of our enemies. The Lord clears away a spot for us—sweeps evil and evildoers out of our path—where he can care for us and minister to us. Psalm 23 describes the reality of this life as we know it. We are not told that the Lord will lead us far from all the turmoil of life and there care for us. God cares for us in the midst of the tumult and noise of trials and dangers and enemies. With danger seeming to threaten on every side, we stand secure in the Lord, the cup of our lives overflowing with his blessings. We don't have to desperately search for God and his care. Rather, we are told his goodness and mercy seek us out; they "follow me all the days of my life." The psalm closes with the promise of the ultimate blessing, the gift of eternal life which we already have begun to live in Jesus Christ: "I shall dwell in the house of the Lord for ever."

Psalm 27 also speaks strongly of the care of the Lord and particularly God's protection against our enemies.

> The Lord is my light and my salvation;
>   whom shall I fear?
> The Lord is the stronghold of my life;
>   of whom shall I be afraid?
>
> When evildoers assail me,
>   uttering slanders against me,
> my adversaries and foes,
>   they shall stumble and fall.
>
> Though a host encamp against me,
>   my heart shall not fear;
> though war arise against me,
>   yet I will be confident.
>   (Ps 27:1-3)

This psalm describes the Lord as a "stronghold." In him we have complete security from our enemies. We are left with no one and nothing to fear. We are safe from evildoers, slanderers, those spiritual and natural enemies that make war against us. Considering all this, we can rightly say, "My heart shall not fear." But this declaration is based on much more than just logic. It comes from a special gift of faith. If you rely on your mind alone to believe in God's omnipotence and his promise of faithfulness to his people, you may have trouble reconciling these unchanging truths with your experience of the hardships of life—our sufferings, the momentary triumphs of wickedness, and the prosperity of those who aren't submitted to God. Your unaided mind's shaky grip on these truths probably won't carry you through an experience of overwhelming danger or hard suffering. To make it stick you need faith. Take the promises of God's protection in faith. Make your declaration, "My heart shall not fear," in faith.

Psalm 27 continues:

> One thing have I asked of the Lord,
>   that will I seek after;
> that I may dwell in the house of the Lord
>   all the days of my life,
> to behold the beauty of the Lord,
>   and to inquire in his temple. (v. 4)

Doublemindedness and divided loyalty erode faith. When we make the Lord the "one thing" that we seek, when we put him above all else in our lives, then we will be able to live a life of exuberant faith. This desire to put God first in our lives is the normal and right response flowing from the gift of faith. As we respond in this way to God's action in our lives, we experience an increase of faith.

The psalm continues:

> For he will hide me in his shelter
>   in the day of trouble;
> he will conceal me under the cover of his tent,
>   he will set me high upon a rock. (v. 5)

Here the Lord is described as a shelter, hiding place, and rock, all of which excite an image of security for us. The idea of a rock—a very large rock—especially teaches us about God as a source of protection and security. A rock carries a sense of permanence. Suppose you were traveling through canyons and ravines in an arid region like Palestine or some parts of the Western United States. A heavy rainstorm in the mountains causes a flash flood. You hear a rumbling in the distance, gradually growing louder as the water rushes down the dry ravine towards you. You remember from a previous trip that a large tree grew about a quarter of a mile away; you might be able to climb to safety. But when you arrive at the spot you find the tree toppled over and riddled with dry rot. Trees have a way of coming and going in the space of a few years. You can't rely on them when you're trying to outrace a flash flood. Then you remember another spot a couple of bends further down the canyon. There a huge rock stands on the sandy floor of the valley. It has probably been there for thousands of years. Surely it will be there today when you need it so badly. A rock is something permanent. It isn't washed away by a spring flood. It doesn't topple over and rot away like a tree. When you need something to climb up on to get out of the way of a flood, or to hide behind when robbers are pursuing you, or to shade you from the blistering sun so you don't die of heat prostration, look for a rock, a big rock. That's the way God is for us—reliable, substantial, always there when we need him. Everything else may fail us but God is our strength and our salvation forever.

The eighth verse of Psalm 27 describes the kind of wholehearted response to God's invitation that should shape each one of our lives: "My heart says to thee, 'Thy face, Lord, do I seek' " (Ps 27:8). When we seek God with all our hearts, nothing can keep us from finding him, for he, in the first place, has set about seeking us out.

The psalm closes with a ringing declaration of faith: "I shall see the goodness of the Lord in the land of the living" (Ps 27:13). We don't have to wait until we die to begin experiencing the Lord's care. We begin here and now to live in him and with him, to live our lives free of fear because we are under the protection of the living God. We should make this declaration of faith in every situation in life. It applies in times of greatest peace and abundance as a word of thanks to God.

It applies in times of tragedy, battle, or want as an affirmation of trust in him. Through the gift of faith you know that because of the Lord you can "be strong, and let your heart take courage" (Ps 27:14).

Perhaps you think you are an exception. "Those words of scriptural encouragement are fine for Christians who start out with a strong gift of faith, but I've been behind the eight ball of fear all of my life," you say. "If I was on top of fear, I could use those scriptural promises to stay there. But I've never even been close to being on top." Look again, my friend. The promises of scripture are bigger and more generous than you might have imagined. The gift of faith and the freedom from fear it brings is just as readily available to a man or woman who has been bullied and trampled and held in bondage by fear throughout life as it is to those who have been able to cope successfully. Psalm 34 tells the story of a down-and-outer who overcame his fears through faith in God:

> I sought the Lord and he answered me,
>   and delivered me from all my fears.
> Look to him, and be radiant;
>   so your faces shall never be ashamed.
> This poor man cried, and the Lord heard him,
>   and saved him out of all his troubles.
> The angel of the Lord encamps
>   around those who fear him and delivers them.
> O taste and see that the Lord is good!

> Happy is the man who takes refuge in him!
> O fear the Lord you his saints,
>   for those who fear him have no want!
> The young lions suffer want and hunger;
>   but those who seek the Lord lack no good
>   thing. (Ps 34:4-10)

If you have a healthy fear of the Lord, all other fears and concerns in life will take on their proper perspective. Fear of the Lord opens us to a life of faith in which we experience courage, confidence, and strength. We will live in righteousness and security, able to defy every fear of physical or spiritual danger. We will be at peace with ourselves and with our fellow men.

Consider the story of the "poor man" in Psalm 34. It is an interesting one. Initially, he must have been in desperate bondage to fear, but somewhere along the line he made a turn of direction and did the one thing that counts: "I sought the Lord." The result was exactly as promised: "He answered me." The poor man traded in the fear that kept him in bondage, for a healthy fear of the Lord which brought him freedom. When he feared other men or natural danger or feared for his reputation or for acceptance and security, he was miserable. When he began to fear the Lord, he was able to experience God as good, and his life became one of freedom and happiness.

The New Testament adds to the promises and encouragements of the Old Testament. Not only

The Shield of Faith 99

does the New Testament tell us that we should be free of fears and anxieties, it even says that it is *wrong* for us to submit to them. The message comes to us very strongly in Jesus' own words in the twelfth chapter of Luke's gospel:

> Therefore I tell you, do not be anxious about your life, what you shall eat, nor about your body, what you shall put on. For life is more than food, and the body more than clothing. Consider the ravens: they neither sow nor reap, they have neither storehouse nor barn, and yet God feeds them. Of how much more value are you than the birds! And which of you by being anxious can add a cubit to his span of life? If then you are not able to do as small a thing as that, why are you anxious about the rest? Consider the lilies, how they grow; they neither toil nor spin; yet I tell you, even Solomon in all his glory was not arrayed like one of these. But if God so clothes the grass which is alive in the field today and tomorrow is thrown into the oven, how much more will he clothe you, O men of little faith. And do not seek what you are to eat and what you are to drink, nor be of anxious mind. For all the nations of the world seek these things; and your Father knows that you need them. Instead, seek his kingdom, and these things shall be yours as well.
> Fear not, little flock, for it is your Father's good pleasure to give you the kingdom.
> (Lk 12:22-32)

Jesus warns us about the problem of anxiety, an undue and fleshly concern for our own welfare. In matters of practical approach to life, anxiety is pretty much the opposite of faith. The gospel passage warns us against anxiety over the basic needs of life, but it has broader application. Many Christians today probably trust God to provide for the basics of life, yet anxiously strive for a lifestyle above and beyond what they actually need. The extras bring a sense of security. Jesus puts the anxiety problem in the right perspective through a bit of ridicule. He points out that such anxiety can't lengthen our lifespan even a tiny bit. What sense then does it make to worry about all these things? Jesus chides the anxious, "O men of little faith!" The men of the world go after the necessities and the extras of life on their own because they don't recognize the care of God. By faith we know that God is caring for us. That should free us of concern for ourselves so that we can invest our lives fully in seeking God and his kingdom. To seek after the things of the world is to trade faith for fear. "This is the victory that overcomes the world, our faith" (1 Jn 5:4).

The tenth chapter of Matthew's gospel reinforces the advice of Psalm 34 to fear the Lord rather than man or other dangers:

> And do not fear those who kill the body but cannot kill the soul; rather fear him who can destroy both soul and body in hell. Are not two sparrows sold for a penny? And not one of them

will fall to the ground without your Father's will. But even the hairs of your head are all numbered. Fear not, therefore; you are of more value than many sparrows. (Mt 10:28-31)

Here Jesus is talking about people who actually have the power to put us to death—in this case probably death for being a Christian. He states that physical death is not to be feared. Rather, our lives should be governed by a healthy fear of the judgment of God. The fear of God's judgment is balanced by an expression of God's loving concern for each of us: "But even the hairs of your head are all numbered." God is described as being concerned for the least of his creatures; we are assured that he holds us in high value indeed.

By now it must be clear that faith has many different dimensions in our lives. It is that gift from God that enables us to recognize the truth about him when we encounter it. It is that gift of God through which we are justified and reconciled to him in Jesus Christ (Rom 5:1). It assures us of the blessings which are ours as part of our inheritance as sons and daughters of God but which have yet to come fully into our lives (Heb 11:1). It is a light that enables us to understand in our minds and our hearts the truth about God. It is a shield with which we turn back the threats and taunts and temptations of the evil one (Eph 6:16). Faith is expressed as a trust in God to protect us, deliver us, and strengthen us. God's promise is absolutely trustworthy; we receive it in faith and it enables us to live the life of faith: " 'I will never fail you nor forsake you.' Hence, we can confidently say, 'The Lord is my helper, I will not be afraid; what can man do to me?' " (Heb 13:5-6).

Jesus calls us to a radical life of faith: "And whatever you ask in prayer you will receive, if you have faith" (Mt 21:22). In time of danger or of need, faith crowds fear out of our lives. Jesus instructed the ruler of the synagogue, upon the report that the man's daughter was dead, "Do not fear, only believe" (Mk 5:36). You can live the kind of life of faith that decisively defeats fear because of the profound basic change resulting from conversion to Christ: "I have been crucified with Christ; it is no longer I who live but Christ who lives in me; and the life I now live in the flesh I live by faith in the Son of God, who loved me and gave himself for me" (Gal 2:20).

From one point of view, faith is a weapon we use to overcome fear. From another point of view, faith is the key to a totally new life in Christ in which fear can maintain no foothold.

But both as weapon and as key to life it is a gift to be taken up and used. In faith, we must act.

SEVEN

Looking Reality in the Eye

ONE OF THE BIGGEST REASONS why many Christians can't effectively use the power that God makes available to them is that they don't face up to those things that are wrong and need correcting in their lives. Another big problem, somewhat the opposite of the first, is that many folks blow the problems they do see—like dangers and fears—all up out of proportion. The first group distorts realities about themselves. The second group distorts realities about their problems.

Suppose you plant a garden, and as the days of spring roll by you watch the different seeds sprout and grow taller and unfold their leaves. You admire the beans and carrots and lettuce as they sprout, but along with the vegetables a healthy growth of pigweed starts to come up. If you are not an experienced gardener, you may decide that the pigweed looks like something else that's going to be good to eat and settle back to wait for it to ripen. Or you might let the weed grow even though you know better, deciding that it won't hurt to let it grow with the other vegetables. Or you may despair and do nothing, knowing that left alone the weed will crowd out the useful things in your garden, but that if you cut it down it will only sprout again; you have a hoe and a spade and the time to cultivate, but you just can't face the fact that something in the garden needs correcting. Your garden will fail unless you're willing to call a spade a spade—or, in this case, a weed a weed—and correct the problem.

Many Christians approach problems of fear in their lives in much the same way. They delude themselves, calling fear a virtue, thinking it harmless, or considering it a weakness that can't be overcome. Many different ploys are used to cover up fear problems. "I just can't handle those people. Everytime I go there I freeze up." "Whenever I hear about all the economic problems in this country, I'm overwhelmed by anxiety—not for myself, but for my family." "I'm quiet and reserved by nature. It's the way God made me, and it's a virtue I prize." "I know I talk too much—I have to. It's my only outlet for my insecurities." "I'm always conservative about everything. It's better than being rash or impulsive." All these are examples of excuses for the bondage of fear.

The first step to overcoming these problems is to face up to them. We need to face the fact that we have traits, habits, and weaknesses that allow different kinds of fear to rule certain areas of our lives. We need to get rid of these fears. They limit our ability to love and serve others, to act righteously, to experience the freedom of our new life in Christ, to relate as we should to the Lord. The Lord wants us to recognize that some of the things that go on inside us are disorders that he wants to change.

Our fears are not just our own problems. They harm other people. If we approach a situation timidly when decisive action is what's needed, then our fears become a problem for others. If we're withdrawn and uncommunicative, we can't maintain the kind of active and open relationships with other people that bring unity and trust to the body of Christ. If our insecurities cause us to talk too much, then we waste valuable time that could be used to communicate about important things in the Christian life.

Rationalizations and excuses don't remedy our fear problems; they bury them out of sight where they can't be dealt with. If you're timid and don't talk very much, it's not right to defend yourself by saying, "Scripture says you ought to be slow to speak." This is misapplying scripture to justify your weakness. Scripture tells us to be slow to speak when that's the right behavior. It does not tell us to be so fearful and insecure that we can't communicate freely when we should. You may be able to list ten good reasons why your life is choked with anxiety, but that doesn't change the fact that God tells us through scripture, "Have no anxiety about anything" (Phil 4:6). That scriptural advice about anxiety—pretty much given as a straight-forward command—is followed by advice on how to overcome anxiety. If anxiety rules your life, that's a sign that you are not standing in faith and using the power of the Holy Spirit to fight against your fears.

It helps to recognize that we tend to rationalize about fear problems because we are ashamed of them or because we lack confidence in our ability to overcome them. Fear problems, like problems of guilt or low self-esteem, are often hard to face up to and tell others about. The reason is that our fears make us afraid. Yet that is precisely why we need to make a special effort to face them. The Holy Spirit empowers us to deal with them; we need to use it to fight our fears. Often they take time to overcome and we may be in for a long fight. Regardless, we need to recognize the enemy and confidently use the power God gives us for as long as it takes to win.

The most obvious reason for pretending to ourselves that we don't have a particular problem is that we are afraid to take it on and to endure the suffering that may be involved in overcoming it. Now that I have (I hope) talked you into facing up to any problem fears that you have, you may find yourself quaking in the shadows of a couple that look ten feet tall and grumble and growl threateningly, feeling twice as afraid as ever before, and saying to me, "Thanks a lot!" I guarantee you that things aren't as bad as they seem. Once again, let's look reality in the eye.

My son Mike, when he was about four years old, asked me one day, "Dad, what's a ghost look like when you pull off the sheet?" I'll bet that at least eighty percent of the fears that blight our lives are fifty-dollar fears caused by five-cent dangers. A very small or even a nonexistent danger can pin you down if it stirs up a big enough fear response. It's a bit like certain pain holds in wrestling. By putting pressure on sensitive spots, a small person can hold a much larger and stronger opponent down. It's the same with fear. When any kind of problem has the upper hand in life it looms over you taller than a mountain; it seems to swallow you up like the abyss of the sea; it crushes you to the ground like an overpowering weight.

I am willing to wager that, held up against the light of understanding, most of your fears will shrink to mole hills, dry up to mere puddles, lighten to burdens which you can easily carry. The most important part of getting this grip on reality comes from God's truth. But ordinary human understanding is a big help in disarming fears, too. The description of fear, where it comes from and how it can work in either good or bad ways, is valuable information that can be put to work within the framework of a Christian perspective to overcome fear problems.

The understanding of fear that I will sketch out now is not a summary of secular wisdom about fear, along with some self-analysis techniques. I have not attempted a balanced and thorough review of the psychology and philosophy of fear; I have simply selected some useful insights. More importantly, however, our purpose is to understand fear in the context of Christian truth. This makes a huge difference. It is reasonable to fear many more things from a worldly point of view than it is in the eternal perspective. If you don't believe in God and eternal life, everything of meaning to you must be experienced or achieved within the span of your life on earth. To lose your life is greatly to be feared, because with it you lose everything. If you don't believe in God, the only resources you have to call upon in your struggle with fear are those of human ones—your own strength and wisdom; the help of friends, counselors, analysts; security that comes from material possessions; pills and medications. If you don't believe in God and the power of the new life into which he calls us through his son, Jesus Christ, then no clear standard exists by which to judge how emotions like fear should or should not work in your life. You may think that your fearfulness is some kind of indelible, unchangeable "way that you are," instead of a result of the misshaping influence of sin and the disorder of a fallen world, something from which a loving God wants to rescue you.

It should be clear from all that has been said so far that the understanding we seek comes from many sources. Part is gathered from God's revealed word in scripture; part from human experience and the wisdom it brings; still another part from studies of man and how he functions. To these must be added an expectant seeking of the Lord for insight into individual fear problems—an openness to revelation from God himself for you, in this particular problem, at this moment in your life. It may not come; it may not be needed. But it often is the key to freedom. And it very often is freely given.

The understanding about fear presented in Chapters One and Two can be summarized in six points:

1. Fear is an automatic response to danger, involving a complicated set of changes in the body which prepare us to cope by "fight," "flight," or "freezing." The emotional state we experience ("feeling afraid") involves our nerves, glands, and ideas of danger.

2. Fear is triggered by a stimulus, either an actual danger like pond ice cracking underfoot or something that often accompanies danger, like a sudden loud noise or an angry word.

3. Some fears are natural and innate. Others are learned or acquired.

4. Some fears that are useful while we are very young become disadvantages if they persist into adulthood. Other kinds of fears which are not innate are very useful to acquire as we grow older. Old fears can be overcome and new ones learned.

5. Spiritual forces of evil can stir up, multiply, or intensify natural fears. They can bring spiritually based fears into our lives. In many

cases it would be realistic to add evil spirits to the list of "nerves, glands, and ideas of danger" that are involved in the emotional state of fear as set forth in the first point above.

6. Most of the fears written about in Old Testament times were of concrete dangers like famine or invading armies. Social fears seem to be the more common kind in the world of today.

Let's apply this understanding to two ordinary examples of problem fears to see how it gives a balanced, realistic view that helps us deal with them. The first is fear of lightning, a concrete danger. The second is fear of being rejected by other people, an example of social fear. In both cases we are talking about problem-level fear — fear so great, or ill-founded, or distorted that it limits us in acting in a normal, free way as sons or daughters of God.

When the thunder rumbles louder and louder and the lightning begins to flash across the sky, many people start to sweat at least a little bit. But let's suppose that you have a real problem with fear of lightning, and whenever a storm approaches you don't just sweat a little bit. You run and hide under the bed.

First of all, lightning poses some measure of danger and an appropriate degree of fear response is understandable. However, the appropriate response to lightning is not to run and hide under the bed. The danger is not great enough, and it isn't necessarily any safer under the bed than elsewhere around the house—or perhaps even outside. Nevertheless, it helps to see that some element of danger is present and some degree of fear response is appropriate—consistent with the first point of our summary of how fear works.

In fact, a sudden loud clap of thunder and a sudden brilliant flash of lightning are examples of stimuli which automatically trigger an innate fear response. The suddenness and intensity of the stimulus, which could come from noises or flashes caused by something other than lightning, quite naturally arouse fear. You are born with these responses (points 2 and 3 of the fear summary); if you take the right action when you experience them, fear is working right in your life. However, because in this example your reaction is to dive under the bed, it is clear that you have either failed to grow out of a pattern that is more common in children or that some bad experience or fearful attitudes have taught you to overreact to lightning.

The truth is that in normal circumstances the danger of being struck by lightning even in the midst of a fairly wild storm is remote. Many people enjoy going outdoors during thunderstorms just to admire the beautiful display of lightning. I remember an occasion as a young boy when my parents had taken the whole family on a fishing trip to a trout river. The river flowed close to a country road and an electrical power line paralleled the stream. During the afternoon a sudden thunderstorm came up and my mother took all us kids into the cabin to get out of the rain. But my dad was fishing at the time and the trout were biting pretty well. He was standing right beside a power pole and remained there casting contentedly throughout the storm. When the clouds rolled on and the sun came back out we all went back to the stream to take up fishing ourselves. We were horrified to see smoke billowing out of an electrical transformer twenty-five feet above my father's head; lightning had struck it during the storm. My father had just kept on fishing, however, and his calm reaction had the effect of reducing my own fear of lightning by a factor of about ten.

My experience is typical of the way most of us outgrow excessive fear of lightning. A boy I know overcame that fear in his early teens when his father pointed out the beauty of lightning during a summer night's storm. Another teenager with the same fear realized one day that God sent showers to make things grow and that, therefore, the storms—which were accompanied by lightning—were something that accomplished great good. His fear then vanished. Still another teenager in studying about electricity in a science class was liberated from his fear of lightning simply by acquiring an understanding of the physical phenomenon. These are all examples of people who were freed from fear by gaining a normal understanding or insight about the cause of it. They got a grip on reality that scaled their fear down to proper size.

Looking Reality in the Eye   113

In another instance a teacher—an older woman—who had been afraid of lightning throughout her life, gradually got freed up as she encouraged some of her timid pupils to handle their own fear of lightning. In the process of evangelizing others with truth and logic she herself overcame an unreasonable fear.

Now let's apply our six-point summary of the understanding of fear to a case of social fear. Suppose you are dominated by an overwhelming fear that people will reject you. This is a perceived social danger rather than a concrete physical danger. Fear of rejection also differs from fear of lightning in that the fear is a general matter of disposition or character formation rather than the automatic physiological response to perceived danger. However, in terms of the first point in the summary of fear an automatic response is involved. You experience both a general ongoing inclination to be afraid that people are going to reject you and also periodic flashes of the specific fear response when you encounter certain people or situations. You feel that stab of fear when you meet a particular individual who you find intimidating or whose esteem you fear losing; or when you are involved in a social situation like a formal party where you lack assurance that you can handle yourself according to other people's expectations.

The stimulus that causes the fear reaction is likely to be much more subtle than in the case of concrete physical danger, and the fears are almost certainly learned or acquired rather than innate (points 2 and 3 of our fear summary). The biggest part of the stimulus is likely to be certain patterns or habits of thought about ourselves and about how other people think of us. Attitudes and expectations rather than loud noises or sudden flashes of light stir up the fear response within us. So far as the physical experience of fear is concerned, nerves and glands are likely to play a smaller role than in the case of physical danger, while ideas of the danger the situation holds are likely to be playing a more prominent role.

Understanding just this much of what is going on may itself help greatly to scale the overwhelming proportion of the experience down to more manageable size. It may also suggest some concrete ways to begin dealing with the problem. Maybe some past experiences of rejection—either real or imagined—are dictating your fear response more than any real danger here in the present. Maybe your thinking about what other people think of you is consistently biased to your disadvantage. Maybe there are some legitimate reasons to expect people to reject you and you might be able to change some of them. If you are running with a hostile, critical crowd, maybe a different circle of friends—Christian friends—would offer you the opportunity to gain acceptance and to overcome your fears. Who is likely to reject you anyway? If they are a certain type of person, it might be a compliment to be rejected by them. It is likely, too, that your fear is fed by some exaggerated assumptions about the consequences of being rejected.

Very young children go through a phase when it is natural for them to fear strangers. That type of innate fear is probably useful in some ways for very young children—it may strengthen primary family bonds and prevent them from wandering off with strangers. On the other hand, if such fears aren't overcome as the child grows older, they increasingly become a disadvantage in social relationships. Some people seem never to develop the ability to trust even close friends, parents, or others in special relationships (point 4 of the fear summary). Others develop such trust and then lose it through some especially damaging experience as life goes on. Such a developmental failure or loss could easily impair a person's ability to confidently relate to other people as an adult. For any number of reasons a person may simply have never developed the confidence, boldness, and courage that are the marks of the Christian—character traits that should develop in each maturing man and woman as a son or daughter of God.

In my experience, the work of evil spirits in stirring up or reinforcing fears is likely to be much more pronounced in the area of social fears than in fear of concrete physical danger. Satan is described in scripture as the accuser of the brethren. He works to isolate Christians from one another, thereby depriving them of the support that God intended us all to experience in Christian life. Social isolation caused by fear that we will suffer the hurt of being rejected is a common work of the Evil One. He wants to bring us under condemnation—self-condemnation and fear of condemnation by the Lord and by other people. Understanding this (point 5) enables us to deal with some of the most subtle and irrational aspects of social fear.

Let us review some of the other facts we know about social fear. We know that God means us to live together and to interact in a variety of kinds of relationships—parents and children, blood brothers and sisters, service and business relationships, relationships as brothers and sisters in the Lord, and other friendships. These strong relationships are founded upon bonds of love, service, loyalty, and affection. But God's intentions for loving and sustaining relationships among human beings are often thwarted by sin—by relationships involving hostility, exploitation, and cruelty.

The bad patterns of relating need not involve overt physical violence. In fact, in our society today they seldom do. However, many forms of communication can have the effect of stirring up a fear reaction between people. We use a variety of ritual gestures such as shaking the fist, raising the hand, or standing to full height. Other signals of threat or aggression are a posture of leaning forward or with feet spread wide apart or with hands on hips. Human beings also communicate with facial expressions which may be signal anger or disdain. Even a totally blank facial expression may leave others vulnerable to fear arising from uncertainty about our disposition or intentions toward them. Words and tone of voice are used to communicate warning and insult. A great deal of subtlety attends much of this communication, and it is entirely possible for a person with a fearful disposition to misinterpret a great deal of it. If someone you may be conversing with suddenly arches their eyebrows, you may interpret the expression as no more than an indication of surprise. Yet if you are fearful and insecure, you might interpret the arching of eyebrows as a sure sign that the other person has suddenly detected some terrible flaw in your human makeup, is shocked beyond words, and will certainly reject you.

A less interpretive and less subtle example would be the use of an obviously severe tone of voice in addressing a person. Perhaps a parent or an employer is correcting someone in their charge. A person inclined toward fear of rejection is likely to be devastated by a pointed and emphatic criticism or correction, while a secure and confident individual would accept the correction without experiencing any threat or damage to their sense of security in the relationship. For many people, misunderstanding or being overly sensitive to the way others communicate through word, gesture, and expression causes problems which need not exist. Understanding such possibilities is an important key to getting free, especially in today's world where social fears are so common (point 6).

Now to make some realistic connections among fear, danger, and our reactions. Many people simply believe that if they become afraid, there must be real danger about. There may be a flood or they will be robbed or people won't like them because they're homely and clumsy. It helps to understand that the emotion of fear does not prove that there is anything to be afraid of. Fear is an emotional reaction. It proves nothing about the danger of flood, robbery, or rejection. People with fear problems need to understand that.

Any intense stimulus, like loud noise or very bright light, normally causes a fear response. Very novel or unfamiliar objects or situations do too. It makes sense that our bodies and minds be prepared to deal with the dangers that might accompany loud noise or bright light or the approach of a stranger (a possible enemy) or a totally strange environment. On the other hand, the loud noise may turn out to be music (it often does today); the stranger may be very friendly; the new environment may contain riches and delights.

Because the event or stimulus that triggers fear in us does not necessarily prove the existence of danger, we need to ask ourselves whether real danger confronts us. Sometimes we are able to size up the situation without reacting on the basis of our fear. But this is not always the best thing to do. If somebody were to throw something at you, you might duck before asking whether it is a sponge rubber ball or a brick. Most of the time the reflex reaction to fear is to be respected. Examining the question of whether real danger is present can always be done conveniently—and in safety—a little later. Many people, if they took the time, would discover that some of their greatest fears are responses to assumed rather than real dangers. Once they understand this, they might find that the fears gradually go away on their own. Sometimes, however, additional help is needed.

A second basic point of understanding is that when real danger does exist, that does not automatically mean we should avoid exposing ourselves to it. If we are to accomplish something in life—and enjoy ourselves in the meantime—we need to accept some reasonable risks. Fear working right warns us of the presence of danger and prepares us to cope with it. Fear does not necessarily indicate that we should avoid accepting the risk of the danger. In fact, almost everything we do in life involves some risk. To get an education we go to school and take a chance on being hit by a car on the way. To enjoy a recreational game of racquetball, we risk losing or being accidently bashed over the head by our opponent's racket. When giving money to a person in need, we increase the risk that we might eventually run short ourselves. When working hard to support a family, we accept extra risks of coming down sick as a result of fatigue. Charity and responsibility call on us to take on such risks at reasonable levels. Yet some people, when warned by fear that they might not succeed in a new job, that they might not be welcomed in a new circle of personal relationships, that the plane might crash on the way to that glorious vacation in Hawaii, always interpret the danger that triggered the fear as a reliable indication that they should not take on the risk.

Another step towards a realistic understanding of fear is to think through the consequences of exposure to the danger. What if the worst possibility really came to pass? What would happen if you did actually flunk that examination; lose your job; experience rejection or great embarrassment? Would the world come to an end? Would many people notice your difficulty? Would history change as a result of the disaster that descended upon you? Would your life change significantly? You often hear people say things like "I'll just die if I don't get invited to Susie's party." That's a figure of speech, of course, but it expresses the intense sense of social rejection that people often feel in such situations. The objective fact is that you simply will not die. Yet, to many people, the experience of shame, embarrassment, or rejection is overwhelmingly painful. Carefully and bravely thinking through the actual consequences can help a great deal in reducing the experience of pain. Oftentimes the actual outcome isn't nearly as bad as we anticipate.

Let me tell you the story of one of the most socially terrifying experiences of my life. When I was about eight years old I served as an altar boy in our church. Our pastor was a very severe, old-fashioned Irishman. All the altar boys were scared to death of him. Our church had two huge ornate light stands—candelabras—which stood on either side of the sanctuary and each of which must have contained fifty or more individual light blubs shaped like candle flames. At the critical moment in solemn ceremonies, one of the altar boys had to go into the sacristy and flip a couple of light switches to turn on the candelabras. When you flipped the switch, the whole sanctuary burst into a holy light. The effect was overwhelming.

The first time I served a major solemn service, the responsibility to light the candelabras at the critical climactic moment fell to me. I trudged out of the sanctuary and into the sacristy. I peered at a switchboard with about a hundred switches which controlled all the lights in the church. Each was numbered. Unfortunately, on this special occasion I had forgotten which two numbers out of the hundred or so turned on the candelabras. I took my best guess, flipped the switches and ran to the sacristy door to peer out into the church. I had turned on the wrong lights. I ran back, chose two different switches, turned the first two off, and threw the next two on. I ran back to the sacristy door again, looked out, and discovered that once again I had turned on the wrong lights. At this point I was overwhelmed by fear—thinking about the consequences when the pastor cornered me after the service. I completely panicked, ran back to the switchboard, and threw one switch after another. Outside in the church sanctuary all the different lights were blinking on and off—including, occasionally, the candelabras themselves—in what was undoubtedly the first solemn church service ever celebrated in our conservative part of the country with psychedelic lighting displays. The effect must have been extraordinary. When I finally exhausted myself throwing switches in my wild panic, I trudged back to my place in the sanctuary consumed with fear, guilt, and shame. I noticed that the pastor's face was very red and the veins in his forehead were bulging. The congregation was stunned. The other altar boys were torn between their fear of the pastor and a nearly overwhelming urge to burst out laughing. I was sure that the end had come for me. "I was a dead man."

To my amazement, nothing ever happened as a result of my panic—neither after the church service nor at any time later. I realize now that our pastor was so absolutely appalled and enraged at the spectacle I created that he could think of nothing to do or to say. The early death which I had anticipated never came to pass. I was not thrown out of the church. I was not even beaten or subjected to verbal rebuke. The very magnitude of my blunder protected me from all possible consequences. My fears soon subsided and I went back to leading a normal life, except that I became something of a folk hero among the school kids my age.

When you think through the consequences of the most threatening prospects that might confront you, you can often master your fear. Do you believe that the Lord will care for you? Do you fully trust in God to act in your best interest? If you do, then you accept the prospect that he will care for you in the way that he wants rather than the way that you might choose. These reflections are the final place that we come to as we trace through the consequences of the most terrible dangers that might confront us. So long as we are living righteous lives as Christians, we can see that the worst dangers that our fears warn us of really have no ultimate power over us. While we welcome the useful warning that our fears bring, they, like the dangers themselves, are really of manageable proportion. "None of us lives to himself, and none of us dies to himself. If we live, we live to the Lord, and if we die, we die to the Lord; so then, whether we live or whether we die, we are the Lord's" (Rom 14:7-8). This is reality.

EIGHT

Tilt the Odds in Your Favor

As WE WORK ON FEAR problems, we must realistically measure our strengths and weaknesses and properly analyze our life situation. However, we should not get too focused on ourselves or our problems. Being a bit businesslike, cold, calculating, and impersonal—and above all, not taking things too seriously—helps to keep us from sinking into a morass of self-concern. Our goal is to put aside our personal weaknesses and failings, overcome our fears, and live a full life of righteousness and loving service.

Often we find we can gain victory over fear as part of normal growth towards maturity. All we need is a little common sense or perhaps a process of purely human trial and error. If you were to reflect back over your life, you could probably recall many examples of small victories over fear which you won as you matured over the years. Whether it's a parent coaching and encouraging a child or an individual disciplining himself over a period of time, many fears which had once been problems either are extinguished or reduced to a level where they no longer limit our lives.

But sometimes we need a more carefully planned and sustained approach to overcome a fear problem. Maybe you find yourself regularly lacking in courage and failing to stand up for what's right in different social situations. Perhaps you take too much concern to protect your own needs or interests at the expense of caring for other people. Maybe you regularly find that you are too shy or timid to step out and relate to people in a friendly, trusting way. Perhaps, as you hear about all the uncertainties and strife in the modern world, you have difficulty trusting in God's protection and fall into a chronic state of anxiety. When these fears hold their ground in your life over a period of years, you have reached a place along that path to Christian maturity where, for the moment, an insurmountable rock slide holds you back. The normal pace of life, the ordinary, everyday wisdom can't carry you past.

Often, what's needed at such a point in life is to deliberately set a plan, accepting for the present the necessity of spiritual battle, but working toward and hoping for an early victory if at all possible. In the meantime, you should expect to experience the Lord present with you as you follow the battle plan. Go confidently and aggressively forward while avoiding introspection and guilt.

Sometimes victory over fear comes quickly. In other cases, it takes a long time to gain full freedom. If so, you have to be prepared to do what is necessary to overcome fear. Often full freedom from fear is gained by piling up a long succession of small but hard-won victories over an extended period of time.

Thinking in terms of setting up a battle plan can help you appreciate the importance of doing everything possible to tilt the odds in your favor. One thing any wise tactician does is to choose the grounds on which the battle will be fought with the greatest of care. Don't get trapped in a box canyon. Be sure your flanks are protected. Dig in where there's a water source so you can hold out against a long seige. Protect against infiltrators. By choosing the grounds of the battle to your advantage you can defeat a stronger enemy. But if he traps you, you may be defeated even by an enemy much weaker than yourself.

In fighting fear you should deliberately shape your life environment to give you every possible advantage over your weaknesses and the attacks of Satan. If you don't have a regular prayer life, you are likely to die of spiritual thirst long before you use up all your ammunition. If you let all kinds of worldly values infiltrate your mind, you will not be able to marshall Christian truth as a weapon in your personal battle against fear. Many people take on job challenges, financial debts, and social commitments they can't possibly handle, experience fear and anxiety as a result, and then feel trapped when they see the need for change. It is difficult to take a less demanding job, more in tune with your abilities, at lower pay, when your life style has put you in debt. People who get into this fix have to take up the battle against fear while trapped in a box canyon.

Putting ourselves in the right spiritual environment is the most important step of all. Of course, it's important to have a good relationship with the Lord even if you have no significant fear problems to deal with. My point here is that a well-balanced spiritual life is a basic practical necessity, a key tactical consideration in the battle against our fears. God himself is the source of the power with which we will achieve victory. Faith, truth, wisdom, strength, healing all come from him through a life of prayer, righteous living, service to God and our brothers and sisters. All the other things we can do to overcome our problems will not work as well, or may not work at all, if our spiritual life isn't in good order.

A question arises here. If our spiritual lives are so important, why do non-Christians and those who aren't very good Christians do as well as they sometimes seem to in handling fears? It is tempting to think that some secular remedy like assertiveness training or one of the many psychological self-help techniques is a simpler, more direct, and less demanding solution to fear than an approach that places such heavy emphasis on our spiritual lives. Financial security, personal power, or social prominence might look like better cures for fear than prayer, scriptural wisdom, and deliverance from the work of evil spirits. I do not pretend to have all the answers to questions like these, but I can offer a few observations about Christian versus worldly approaches to fear.

For one thing, some people who have not heard the gospel live honestly and righteously according to their consciences—"what the law requires is written on their hearts" (Rom 2:14-16). The Lord may be active in their lives just as in those who have heard the gospel. However, many nonbelievers do not really banish fear. Some replace bondage to fear with bondage to pride or aggressiveness. Others achieve a false sense of security by accumulating possessions or by keeping themselves thoroughly distracted by the things of the world—career advancement, the social whirl, eating and drinking, intellectual achievement, entertainment and the media, sports and hobbies. Many of these things are not bad in themselves, but none of them should be allowed to take the place of a good relationship with the Lord. The sense of security they provide is part of the "prosperity of the wicked" which Psalm 73 warns can evaporate in an instant. "For they have no pangs; their bodies are sound and sleek. They are not in trouble as other men are; they are not stricken like other men" (Ps 73:4-5). These are the people of the world as the psalmist at first sees them. But the Lord gives him an understanding of their true state: "How they are destroyed in a moment, swept away utterly by terrors!" (v. 19). Genuine and lasting freedom from fear—a freedom that is in harmony with Christian character traits like gentleness, meekness, humility, generosity—comes only from God.

Another part of our life environment that needs to be properly shaped is our thought life. One serious mistake many Christians make is to give all kinds of inputs from the world free access to their minds. Often we give these inputs equal standing alongside the truths that come from God. One result is that we hear a lot about the world around us that causes or feeds fears. Another result is that an excessive amount of "news" undermines the mind's ability to use truth to overcome fear.

Suppose you faithfully watch a half-hour TV news program every night, spend fifteen minutes scanning the newspaper every day, then spend a half hour each week with a news magazine. That adds up to a little more than five-and-a-half hours per week given to absorbing "news"—not an unusual amount. I am sure many people spend much more time than that. Suppose too that you spend one hour per week reading God's word in scripture. I am sure many people do much less than that. This means you hear five times more about wars, murders, economic crises, political corruption, technological breakthroughs, sports, and social change than you do about the gospel, that God loves and cares for you, that repentance and faith in Jesus Christ bring us to eternal life, and that the world is passing away. If the good news gets crowded out of your thoughts by the bad news, it is small wonder that you are easy prey to fear. This doesn't mean that you shouldn't keep abreast of important happenings in the world about you, or that you should retreat from the realities of life. It does mean that God's eternal, unchanging truth should occupy the prime place in your thought life, that all the information from the world should be made subject to and be tested by this truth, and that you should be selective about how much and what kinds of thoughts and ideas you accept.

I know of people who are very afraid of the possibility of perishing in a nuclear war, but who haven't the slightest concern over the possibility of going to hell when they die. Now, nobody wants to be turned into a radioactive cinder, but even if this happens it is only a temporary condition. Why aren't these people more concerned about their final, permanent state? Probably because they are much more tuned in to news about the first possibility than to news about the second. They are so preoccupied by the fear of a *possible* reckoning with a nuclear explosion that they neglect to consider a *certain* reckoning with God at judgment. An individual can do little on his own to eliminate the nuclear danger and the fear it creates. Yet each man and woman can do a great deal to prepare for impending judgment by accepting God's invitation to repent and believe. If we invest our thoughts in God, we will do better both in this life and the next.

Scripture holds a wealth of wisdom about using our minds in the right way. Psalm 112 says of the man who fears the Lord, "He is not afraid of evil tidings; his heart is firm, trusting in the Lord. His heart is steady, he will not be afraid" (vv. 7-8). Remember that in biblical times the heart was considered to be not only the seat of the emotions, but the seat of thought, intelligence, attention. The message of the psalm would be just as well expressed in terms of a man whose mind is steady, whose thoughts are orderly because he has God's wisdom. This is the man who is not afraid, even in the face of evil tidings. The admonition in Colossians 3:2 is straightforward: "Set your minds on things that are above, not on things that are on earth." And Paul elaborates in his letter to the Philippians: "Whatever is true, whatever is honorable, whatever is just, whatever is pure, whatever is lovely, whatever is gracious, if there is any excellence, if there is anything worthy of praise, think about these things. What you have learned and received and heard and seen in me, do; and the God of peace will be with you" (4:8-9).

Your plan to fight fear must include a realistic assessment of your circumstances and expectations. Some changes might be in order. Many people ought to be afraid, considering the dangers they face, but it's their own fault that those dangers are hanging over them. They have put themselves in situations in life which they can't handle. Each of us has our limits. If we get in over our heads we usually experience fear of failure, constant anxiety, feelings of inadequacy. I once worked with a man who was head of an important department in a very large corporation. He knew his work well enough, but lacked confidence and personal authority. He became very fearful in the face of his heavy responsibilities. His fears caused some serious physical problems, but he hung on anyway. Eventually things got so bad that the vice-president brought in a new department head and transferred my acquaintance into a new, non-challenging job. The company probably should have fired him, but he had been reduced to such a shambles by his fears that the shock of being fired might have killed him.

I know a lady, a responsible Christian woman, who isn't satisfied with living within her husband's modest but adequate income. In order to have more luxuries in life, she has been holding down a full-time job for some years. She has been careful to meet the needs of her family while working outside the home, but the pace of life has become so demanding that she suffers constantly from anxiety and nervousness. This is a problem in itself, but it also makes it much harder for her to cope with the normal problems and challenges that come along in raising a family. This mother is overtaken by fear and worry if one of her children, who are now well into their teens, has difficulty with their studies or becomes a bit rebellious. If the pace of life were slower, she could confidently handle these problems; she did so in the past.

One of my biology professors in college was a congenial man of moderate intelligence and still more moderate ambition. He was a good teacher but a total failure as a researcher. Yet his wife had a burning ambition for his social and career advancement and prodded him mercilessly. That's probably why he got a job at a major university where the department chairman pressured him to do brilliant research. The professor was afraid of his wife and afraid of his boss. He felt inadequate and insecure. Life was miserable. He escaped both his wife and his boss by suddenly dying of a heart attack before the age of fifty.

The lesson to be drawn from these stories is a simple one: we should shape our lives so that we are not under unnecessary pressure to operate beyond our abilities. These pressures cause a variety of fear problems themselves and so disorder our lives that we have difficulty overcoming fears that arise from other sources.

We should realize that life has a rhythm and learn with experience how to take on greater and greater challenges. I remember tackling several very challenging jobs on a short-term basis when just starting out in my career. I handled them well enough but experienced a lot of pressure and found my confidence stretched to the limit. I doubt that I could have handled the demands they placed on me over a long period of time—say for several years. In any event, some years later, with the benefit of more experience and maturity I handled much more difficult jobs for long periods of time without any difficulty.

The final part of a battle plan to overcome fear has to do with forming strong, supportive personal relationships. God created us as beings who are meant to have meaningful, enduring relationships with families, relatives, friends, and neighbors, relationships through which we serve others and are ourselves sustained. Isolation from meaningful human relationships usually leaves us vulnerable to fear. It is also true that close personal relationships, especially Christian relationships, are one of the most effective helps in overcoming many different fear problems, particularly social fears.

Modern life works against personal relationships in many ways. Affluence and mobility, advantages in some ways, often promote the breakup of family and friendship ties. It is common for people to move from one end of the country to the other for a better job, a change of scenery, or milder climate. Employers transfer their workers with little regard for the effect on people's lives. Furthermore, traditional Christian values such as loyalty, respect, trust, and unselfish service play a much smaller part in human affairs than in the past. As a result we cannot take it for granted that the relationships we fall into in the ordinary course of life will protect us from fear and will help us overcome those fears we already have.

They should ideally possess all those qualities

presented in scripture as the qualities of a mature man or woman of God. They should a reflect the character of God himself, in whose image and likeness they are created. Our lives should be influenced and supported by Christian men and women who richly bear the fruit of the Holy Spirit (Gal 5:22-23), who are living examples of the beatitudes (Mt 5:3-12). Men should be of the spiritual stature of Job (Job 29) and women of surpassing excellence like the good wife of Proverbs 31. It is the gift of God's own love that infuses relationships among human beings with the power to strengthen weaknesses, heal wounds, and free from bondage. The love and respect we receive from brothers and sisters in Christ give us strength and confidence to deal with our own problems. In a very real way, their strength becomes our strength. Blessed by their openness and patience, we gradually are drawn along by their example to greater faith and courage. If you want to put yourself in an environment where you can effectively work to overcome problems of fear, put yourself in well-balanced, committed relationships with mature men and women of God.

A well-balanced set of relationships is not likely to be found just within a narrow circle of family members or friends. We would hope for healthy bonds between husband and wife, parents and children. But strong ties among mature Christian men and among Christian women are also essential. God also wants us to have ties with pastors, leaders, family elders, teachers, and others who can bring the Lord's authority and wisdom into our lives. Forming these relationships is a key part of shaping our life environment so that we take up the fight against problems like fear with the odds tilted in our favor.

NINE

Direct Attack on Problem Fears

OUR EMOTIONS ARE SUPPOSED to be our servants, not our masters. They should operate in such a way that they support us in thinking and acting righteously. Fear should physically prepare us to fight off a danger or to escape it, whichever is the right response. Anger should help us to express the seriousness of another's wrongdoing, to fight effectively against an evil or an enemy, or to serve the Lord with dedication and zeal. When operating in these ways our emotions are our faithful servants. However, if our fears overwhelm us and lead us to cowardice or to social isolation, or if our anger leads us to sin in speech or to physically harm another person, then those emotions have become our masters. They, rather than standards of righteousness, are directing our thoughts and actions.

When our emotions aren't working right we can take direct steps to master them and bring them into good order. Dealing with unruly emotions can be something like a lion taming act, or at least like discipline training for a pet dog. We need to bring authority to bear to quell rebellion and establish good habits. One way to do this is to discipline ourselves to think and act in the right way despite our wayward emotions. Over a period of time our emotions will gradually begin to flow in appropriate channels that support correct patterns of thought and action. Think and act rightly and your emotions will learn to follow. This is just ordinary, everyday training, and it works great when applied to emotions like fear.

If you are afraid to meet a certain person, worried about the state of the economy, lack confidence in your latest job assignment, or fear that you will not be able to meet the needs of your family, you have time to evaluate the danger which the fear warns about before choosing a right course of action. But where some imminent danger triggers a reflex fear response—you duck when somebody throws a brick at you or you jump when you hear a sudden loud noise—then the thing to do is react instantly and later take time to consider whether the reaction was appropriate. Either way, we can shape our reactions to fear by figuring out what's right to do, sometimes over an extended period of trial and error, and getting in the habit of doing it.

Several chapters back I described my fear of meeting my college professors when I was a freshman. I pushed past that fear to make the contacts that would enable me to get the most out of my education. As over the following years I repeatedly did the thing I was afraid to do, the fear reaction gradually subsided. By regularly thinking and acting in the right way, my irrational and unruly emotions got starved out. Had I continued to submit to them, they probably would have strengthened their control over me. Doing the right thing becomes a habit after enough repetition, and the habit of doing right becomes stronger than the emotion of fear. In addition, doing right brings many tangible rewards, both spiritual and material. Making necessary contacts with my teachers brought me a better education. Extending yourself to make new friends brings the reward of companionship, affection, and the opportunity to serve others in meaningful ways.

Several practical steps can be taken to help in beginning the training process in the face of problem fears. First, remind yourself that the Lord's love and protection are with you and are much greater than any danger that might confront you. Second, don't allow yourself to react to your fears without first weighing the situation. Don't let them stampede you. Third, ask the question: is the perceived danger real? If the answer is no then go right ahead and do the right thing in the situation. If the answer is yes then ask, "Should I take the risk?" If you should take the risk, do so if you can. If your fear is so great that you can't take on the risk even though you know it's the right thing to do, then calmly and dispassionately try to figure out how you can overcome the fear. Maybe you can't do it on that one occasion, but you can anticipate a repetition of the pattern. You can gradually develop an approach to conquering your fears.

Get in the habit of taking these steps. They might at first sound like a long drawn-out process, one that would require five minutes of reflection and deliberation at the onset of each fear. Actually they all can be condensed into a nearly instantaneous process. For example, if you believe it is right to get up and share something about your life at a meeting of a group of Christians that you are part of but you feel inhibited by fear, then simply learn to do the following. Recall that God loves you; that you are in the company of committed friends; that you can serve them by what you have to share; that your brothers and sisters are not going to hold it against you if you do not speak well; and, furthermore, "you did not receive the spirit of slavery to fall back into fear, but you have received the spirit of sonship" (Rom 8:15). The very first time you should be able to run those reflections through your mind in no more than one second. Don't be surprised if while you're doing it someone else begins to speak and you miss your opportunity to get up and share. You will probably experience the lost opportunity as a welcome relief. The next time the chance comes your way you should be able to run that same string of reflections through your mind in three-quarters of a second. You can get on top of the fear well enough with those truths that you can get to your feet and begin to share with your brothers and sisters. As you keep training yourself you will find that a social situation will trigger the fear which will trigger your instantaneous recitation of truth, which will diminish the fear which will free you to act in an appropriate way. As truth gets a firmer grip on your life, the hold of fear will weaken. As you face fear repeatedly and see that you aren't harmed, the fear will gradually die out.

Sit down and make a list of different experiences in life which at first caused you to fear but which later became tolerable and even enjoyable. The first time you jumped into deep water; the first time you visited away from home overnight; when you first fought a bigger kid or gave a speech before a class or flew in an airplane or were lost in the woods or attended a big party. How many times since have you gone swimming or flying or travelling or spoken to groups or attended parties without the least tremor of fear? Probably a mix of training and a deepening understanding were involved in gaining freedom. It is natural that we grow in confidence, courage, and boldness as we successfully handle new kinds of experiences. This same process of training by repeatedly encountering and handling fearful situations that occurs naturally and spontaneously in many areas of our lives can be deliberately and purposefully pursued as a means of dealing with problem fears.

We should not let fear keep us from doing what is right. Problem fears are problems for us because they limit our enjoyment of a full and meaningful Christian life. They are also problems for others, who are deprived of our service or who must take on our weaknesses and inadequacies as their own burdens. Social fears and anxious concerns are particularly destructive because they attack the relationships among the members of the body of Christ, who should be bound together in love and service. We are not intended to lead our lives as isolated individuals, but we cannot effectively lead the kind of shared life that the Lord intends if we are limited by social fears. It is tragic when husband and wife are limited in their ability to serve one another by fears which inhibit them and plague their relationship, or when parents are so imprisoned by their fear that they cannot effectively form and direct their children. God's people cannot prosper when our efforts to share our abundance with the needy are hindered by fear of inconvenience, sacrifice, or physical danger. If we fear our loss of independence we will have difficulty submitting to God and making commitments to one another. Some men and women are so afraid of losing their independence that they find it difficult to take on the responsibilities that marriage and family life entail.

Since many of our fears were trained into us, it stands to reason that we can train them back out. A powerful part of the message conveyed to us through the media orients us toward consumerism and self-gratification. Repeated exposure to such messages has the effect of training us to fear the loss of things which gratify us. Many people are trained at an early age into the form of fear called "self-concern." Overprotective parents may incessantly caution their children: "Be careful or you'll get hurt"; "Don't get wet or you'll catch cold." Many people in today's world are taught to perform and achieve in order to gain approval and to confirm their sense of self-worth. We are taught that we need to have fine clothes, excellent food, and a grand house in order to be happy and secure. We are told that if we don't eat a precisely balanced diet with the full complement of vitamins, minerals, and trace elements, something very bad—though usually vaguely defined—will happen to us. Messages of these kinds tend to train us in self-concern. It is also often true that if we express fear, others reward us with consolation, protection, and indulgence, which casts us into still deeper bondage. All these experiences are examples of training to be fearful. But the training can be reversed; we can overcome our fears.

Another canoeing story comes to mind. The wildest stretch of the normally placid river near our home is a fifty yard rapid at an abandoned mill site, which provides some moderate white water during spring runoff. Before we made the white water run in the Montana River that I described earlier, it used to be something of a thrill to go through this stretch of rapids near home. I was running it one spring with my son Paul when he chuckled and told the following story. "Sometimes when I float this stretch with my friends for the first time they get so scared that they drop their paddles and grab hold of the sides of the canoe and hold on for dear life." He chuckled again. "I could never do that. When I was first learning to canoe the river Mike or Tom [two of his older brothers] would reach up and bash me over the head with their paddles if I looked like I was getting scared enough to drop my own." He chuckled again.

That might not be the most gentle way to get trained out of fear but at least it's effective. What if his brothers had indulged Paul when he showed the normal signs of fear on the rapids? They could have eased him to shore and said "Oh, that's all right, Paul. It's understandable that you'd be so afraid that you'd drop your paddle. I just hope that you'll outgrow it as you grow older." A liberal dose of sympathy, indulgence, and tolerance would probably have taught Paul to allow his actions to be dictated by fear. Instead he got trained to do the right thing despite his fear. When you're running the rapids the thing to do is to paddle like crazy. If you freeze up, drop your paddle, and grab the sides of the canoe, it's a lot harder for your partner to handle the run safely, and you're a lot more likely to get dunked in the river. It's better to get swatted over the head with a paddle a couple of times than to be trained to surrender to fear and do the wrong thing.

One of the best ways to train ourselves to act in the right way is to simply imitate Christian men and women who have overcome fear in their own lives and who exhibit the virtues of confidence, boldness, and courage. By observing such people, we can learn what to fear and what not to fear. If our own emotions do not provide us with a reliable indication, then it may be easier to learn from the well-tuned judgments and emotional reactions of mature Christians.

We can learn quite a bit by simple observation about how to behave in such a way that fears can be overcome. If we have trouble dealing with strangers or unfamiliar social situations, we should watch how mature men and women, non-Christians as well as Christians, handle themselves in those same situations. We will probably discover that mature, well-balanced people are almost always warm, engaging, open, confident, and considerate in relating to others. We will probably see quickly that they focus their attention on others and seem quite at ease and relatively oblivious to themselves. These people do not have some rare and unique gift which is inaccessible to us. We should simply learn to imitate the way they behave and begin to act in the same way in the social situations that cause us to be afraid. Our first attempts at imitation may be strained, but people will respond well as we increasingly focus away from ourselves and on others. With only a little practice any normal person can learn to relate socially in an acceptable way. Each small success in relating to other people builds confidence, and our confidence helps us relate still more successfully on succeeding occasions.

As we practice the right way of relating, we will learn that our behavior doesn't have to be perfect in order for others to warmly accept us. By imitating other mature Christians, we train ourselves to do the right thing in spite of our fears. We gradually train our emotions to support rather than obstruct right Christian relating.

This whole idea of training has a scriptural basis. God himself rewards good and punishes evil. He does this to administer justice, but also to train us in paths of righteousness. Many of the passages in scripture which deal with training refer to it in terms of "discipline." This often means some form of punishment or correction, but it regularly refers also to training in the broader sense. "Discipline" in scripture means being formed and directed by having the right ways to think and act pointed out to us, by being trained to repeatedly follow righteous ways, and imitating mature Christians.

St. Paul tells us in his letter to the Romans that "suffering produces endurance, and endurance produces character, and character produces hope" (5:3-4). This passage can be applied to the difficult process of dealing with problem fears. "Suffering" is involved in taking on hard things in our lives—like facing up to our fears. But facing up to hard things, and doing it again and again, makes us stronger internally; it "produces endurance." This makes us better men and women, more the people God intends us to be; "endurance produces character." And "character produces hope." We come more and more fully into our inheritance as his sons and daughters; all the fruits of salvation, our new life, and freedom from fear become more and more ours. What's more, when you face up to fears you almost always discover that you have less to fear than you thought.

All the natural, practical ways of dealing with problem fears that have been described so far in this and earlier chapters should be prayerfully used and, in a sense, are filled with spiritual power. That is, God works through them. Understanding how emotions work, being realistic, standing on truth, being tactically wise, and training ourselves are basic parts of normal Christian life, not specific spiritual approaches to fear problems. Now, however, we come to three additional and powerful helps in overcoming fear problems: deliverance, healing, and repentance. These might be seen as specific spiritual ministries. They bring spiritual authority to bear against our fears. Christians today often seize on deliverance and healing as the sole or most important means to deal with significant problems, but they are actually most effective when used in conjunction with the practical steps we have been discussing. This fact disappoints some Christians. Who wouldn't rather be delivered instantly and effortlessly through a brief prayer uttered by a faith-filled friend instead of having to submit to three years of personal discipline to train yourself out of habitual fears? Yet the pathway to freedom is likely to be prescribed by God, not left to our personal preference, and God regularly calls us to submit to painful discipline and to struggle with our weaknesses even as he freely imparts special graces such as deliverance and healing.

The lesson from experience is that the Lord works when we do our part. We are not expected to overcome our problems unaided, but neither does the Lord—for the most part—want us to passively wait for him to do it all for us. Rather, we are to tackle our weaknesses and problems in cooperation with the grace that he supplies. One of the most effective ways to use deliverance, healing, and repentance in dealing with fear problems is to call them into play when a person who has been making good use of other available means seems to have arrived at a plateau in life where further progress is stalemated. These ministries often have the effect of removing the spiritual obstacle that has caused the stalemate, enabling the person to proceed to a new phase of growth.

One of Jesus' major public ministries was delivering people from bondage to evil spirits. He commissioned his disciples with the same authority, and deliverance today is an important means of dealing with spiritual problems. Jesus sent the seventy disciples out with a commission to preach the gospel and to heal the sick. Upon their return they rejoiced in the power that the Lord had given them over the works of Satan in people's lives. Jesus confirmed the grant of power: "Behold, I have given you authority to tread upon serpents and scorpions, and over all the power of the enemy; and nothing shall hurt you. Nevertheless, do not rejoice in this, that the spirits are subject to you; but rejoice that your names are written in heaven" (Lk 10:19-20). In one of the last commissions given his followers on earth, Jesus said, "And these signs will accompany those who believe: in my name they will cast out demons" (Mk 16:17).

Christians today can exercise the same kind of authority over the work of evil spirits in their lives. Sometimes the presence of evil spiritual influences is obvious from natural observation. Signs of the work of the evil one include irrational, bizarre, and complusive fears; unwarranted social fears which isolate Christian men and women from trusting relationships; and anxieties that seem to color every aspect of a person's life. If the work of evil spirits is not the primary cause of such conditions, it is almost certain to be present as a reinforcing component of the problem fear. Constellations of associated fears are often present. Anxiety, insecurity, confusion, pessimism, hopelessness may operate in concert in a person's life so that it is difficult or impossible to tell whether one type of fear or many—or one spirit or several—is at work. Often the Lord will reveal something about these workings of evil. Through his power we can often identify otherwise obscure workings of evil spirits in order to take spiritual authority over them and to take practical steps to undo the fears they cause. Deliverance is usually thought of as an appropriate spiritual means of dealing with various degrees of oppression and bondage caused by evil spirits. Cases of possession, in which the devil exercises complete control over a person, are dealt with through formal exorcism. The normal approach in deliverance is simply to take authority over the workings of evil spirits by a pronouncement such as "In the name of Jesus Christ, I command you, spirit of fear, to depart."

Fear, like other spiritual maladies, may inflict deep hurts upon a person. Psychological, spiritual, and mental suffering commonly result from prolonged or intense encounters with disorders like fear. These wounds should be healed.

Sometimes there is little practical distinction between the ministries of deliverance and healing when used to deal with a fear problem. Nonetheless, there are cases in which we clearly should call on the Lord as our healer. In the gospels, Jesus often ministers through physical healing, as well as through deliverance. Psalm 34 tells us, "When the righteous cry for help, the Lord hears, and delivers them out of all their troubles. The Lord is near to the brokenhearted, and saves the crushed in spirit. Many are the afflictions of the righteous; but the Lord delivers him out of them all" (vv. 17-19). And Psalm 147 says, "He heals the brokenhearted, and binds up their wounds" (v. 3). If a person suffers from the deep and lasting imprint of some terrifying experience, then we should seek the Lord in faith-filled prayer to heal him or her of that affliction. Sometimes an experience such as abandonment by a parent at an early age may live on to torment a person. These wounds can be caused by real or imagined dangers; by concrete situations or intense fantasies. I have pastored people who experienced a moment of overwhelming fear early in life which left a permanent shadow of depression, anxiety, or anticipation of doom. Prayer for healing often brings great relief from such burdens.

Repentance is a third spiritual weapon to use against fear problems. Repentance is often thought of as remorse for wrongdoing, but it is more fundamentally an acknowledgement of our sin, a plea for God's forgiveness, and a decision to turn away from that wrongdoing. "For godly grief produces a repentance that leads to salvation and brings no regret" (2 Cor 7:10); "I acknowledged my sin to thee, and I did not hide my iniquity; I said, 'I will confess my transgressions to the Lord'; then thou didst forgive the guilt of my sin" (Ps 32:5). A key element of repentance is a decision to turn away from the pattern of wrongdoing and to embrace patterns of righteousness. The decision to change is up to the repentant sinner. The strength to make the decision and to change our lives is a gift from God. Repentance is so strongly associated with wrongdoing in most of our minds that we would probably not think of repenting of a problem with fear. Often, however, that is exactly what is needed to launch a person on the road toward freedom. Making a personal decision before God to turn away from patterns of surrender to fear and seeking God for the strength to overcome fear problems is repentance. We can fruitfully repent of the pattern of fear itself, our surrender to fear, and our passive acceptance of an image of ourselves as "fearful people."

Deliverance, healing, and repentance often work well in concert with one another because oppression by evil spirits, hurts and sufferings, and some degree of surrender to our problems are often intertwined in subtly reinforcing ways. An intense experience of fear can inflict a lasting hurt and provide an opening for the working of evil spirits; the wound of fear and the active multiplication of fears under the influence of evil spirits can unfold into an increasingly complex pattern of bondage. Such a pattern often begins when the victim is relatively young and limited in his or her ability to counter the fear problem. By the time they have grown old enough to face their difficulties, they may well have lost the resolve to deal with them. People in this situation can expect God to visit their lives repeatedly with special opportunities to gain freedom from bondage to fear. Often he will do this through deliverance, healing, and repentance.

The Lord works through these ministries in many different ways. One of the most effective ways to experience their power is the "do it yourself" approach. Whether you are dealing with a momentary fear or are waging an ongoing battle to overcome some significant fear problem, it is entirely possible, practical, and desirable for you to turn to the Lord at any time to ask that by his power you be delivered from the oppression of evil spirits, healed from the trauma that fears have impressed upon you, or be forgiven for some wrong that you are responsible for. Your God is always close at hand, offering you new life, victory, and freedom. On the other hand, it is often a very helpful to seek the support of other Christian men and women, particularly those to whom God has invested special gifts of ministry. You might enlist their aid in a moment of specific difficulty or for an ongoing program aimed at overcoming serious fear problems. You might be ministered to by an ordained clergyman of your church, a personal friend, a spiritual confidant, or a counselor. The wisdom, perspective, faith, and experience of others is often a tremendous help to us in opening our lives to the full effect of the power of God. In some Christian traditions, deliverance, healing, and repentance are ministered through formal sacraments. For example, the Catholic sacrament of reconciliation contains elements of all these ministries, although repentance is the main focus.

The quick and easy way to overcome a fear is to be freed miraculously and effortlessly by a sovereign act of God. This is great when it happens, but more often the Lord doesn't work in quite that way. Most commonly God's miraculous intervention is mixed with a full measure of human cooperation. Some fifteen years ago I had a fairly large family, a wife and young children who were very much dependent upon me and the income I provided. We lived in a part of the country many hundreds of miles from where we had grown up and where most of our relatives and early friends still lived. As my family responsibilities grew, I was gradually overtaken by anxiety over what would happen to them if I should be disabled or suddenly die. It seemed that no guarantee existed for their care or security. I didn't actively worry about this, but I did experience a gnawing concern and anxiety. However, when I was baptized in the Holy Spirit, that anxiety instantly and completely vanished from my life. I didn't ask the Lord to take it away or get somebody to pray over me for deliverance; it simply vanished after I was baptized in the Holy Spirit. I just got free grace. Theologically speaking, all grace is free—that's what the very word means—but in this case grace just happened because I had accepted the Lord in a far deeper way than ever before. However, God doesn't always remove our problems in this way—even if we are the most trusting, faith-filled, and righteous Christians in the world. Getting free from problem fears more often involves forcing ourselves to confront them. There seems to be some important connection between doing our part and receiving God's help. Maybe the right way to think about it is that grace in all cases is freely given, but we often have to do something to be able to soak it up.

Rarely will only one of the practical steps we have discussed be enough by itself to overcome fear in our lives. Usually several different approaches working together will bring freedom. The right mix of understanding, repentance, deliverance, relationships, confronting and disarming fears, and imitating mature Christian men and women will depend on the particular problem that confronts us. Often we will need to understand how character traits such as caution or conservatism work in our lives. If we are cowardly, repentance is likely to be in order. Being in strong supportive relationships with other Christians is likely to be essential in overcoming social fears such as timidity, reserve, and insecurity.

Suppose you have a problem with anxiety. The problem may have started with an early life experience in which you were subject to severe disappointment or exposed to some situation which made you very insecure. This experience might have provided opportunities when evil spirits began to work in a significant way in your life. Thus deliverance might be a first step to freedom. But you might also need to understand how certain situations in your life stir those anxieties in a particularly strong way. You might then plan measures to avoid those situations—for example, by disciplining yourself to minimize exposure to anxiety-producing economic news or to anxious friends who communicate their anxiety to you. You probably also need to grow in faith—entrusting yourself to the Lord and founding your life more securely on his truth. Along with all this, you might deliberately seek out a circle of Christian friends who are confident and optimistic and who will give you an opportunity to become trained in right and healthy attitudes and patterns of behavior.

The emphasis in this chapter has been on practical human and spiritual approaches by which problem fears can be directly attacked. Again I caution against the impression that we overcome our problems by our own unaided efforts, or that there is a set of purely natural processes—apart from God's loving care—which is the key to freedom. God works both miraculously in our lives and through a whole array of natural formative processes. It's *his* power that works through miraculous interventions that bring us freedom, and *his* power that works through natural pathways. It is up to us to dispose ourselves and to cooperate freely so that the power of God can work profoundly in our lives. Ultimately, it is he who will bring us to the full freedom of the sons and daughters of God, "to mature manhood, to the measure of the stature of the fullness of Christ" (Eph 4:13).

TEN

A Fighting Spirit

YOU CAN TAKE all the right steps, technically speaking, to reach some important goal in life, and still fall short. There's something in *how* you do a thing that often makes the difference—something to do with determination, drive, enthusiasm. We can speak of it as the *spirit* in which we take on a challenge. In taking on all that life brings our way—and in nothing does this apply more directly than in dealing with fear—the Lord wants his sons and daughters to have a fighting spirit. We don't have to accept weaknesses in our character any more than we have to put up with habits of sin. As we fight these weaknesses, we need to strike the right balance. On the one hand, we must entrust ourselves to the Lord and go to him as a refuge and source of strength. On the other hand, we should take an active, militant role in using the power of God to deal with our problems. Some people cast their problems upon the Lord but fail to do their part to overcome them. Others make the mistake of trying to solve all their problems through their own strength and fail to rely on the power of God. Entrusting ourselves to the Lord is faith; actively working to overcome our problems is fight. Faith and fight work hand in hand to overcome problems like fear in our lives.

In writing to Timothy, Paul exhorts him: "Fight the good fight of the faith; take hold of the eternal life to which you were called when you made the good confession in the presence of many witnesses" (1 Tm 6:12). To have the faith of a Christian means to take on a fighting spirit. Christians are expected to fight for the kingdom of God; to fight against temptation, sin, and evil; to fight against weaknesses like fearfulness in our own character. We are to fight against everything that is an obstacle to the fullness of salvation coming into every area of our lives. Paul's instruction to Timothy shows clearly that faith leads to action, not passivity. In addition to the exhortation to fight, Paul also tells Timothy to "take hold" of eternal life. When God gives gifts like faith and eternal life to his sons and daughters, we aren't to receive them passively. These gifts are not just dumped on us. We take hold of them and we use them.

In his second letter to Timothy, Paul gives advice that enlarges our understanding of a Christian fighting spirit: "Hence I remind you to rekindle the gift of God that is within you through the laying on of my hands; for God did not give us a spirit of timidity but a spirit of power and love and self-control" (2 Tm 1:6-7). Paul uses action words—"rekindle the gift of God"—that is, stir up that gift of power that God has implanted within you. You have received a gift of the Holy Spirit—power that enables you to love others and to control the way you act. The Lord wants us to live our Christian lives through the power of the Holy Spirit. This power, not our fears or other weaknesses, should control how we act. We can be sure that the power of God is greater than the power of fear; for that reason, we can control ourselves in such a way as to do right regardless of which direction our emotions pull us in. We are able to act confidently not because of our own strength but because of the power of God within us. His power enables us to fight off our fears.

This reliance on God's power through the right balance of faith and fight is well illustrated in Psalm 18—one of the most militant of the psalms. The Lord is addressed as rock, fortress, deliverer, refuge, shield (v. 2). The psalmist vividly describes his helplessness (vv. 4-5). The Lord's response is to save the man from his hopeless straits: "He drew me out of many waters. He delivered me from my strong enemy and from those who hated me; for they were too mighty for me" (vv. 16-17). In short, the first part of the psalm describes a hopeless and helpless human being bound hand and foot by his enemies and being swept away to sure destruction in a swelling current of evil power. Then the Lord in awesome might reaches out to sever the bonds of the helpless victim and to gently lift his limp and battered body to safety. You might picture the

Lord giving the man the spiritual equivalent of artificial respiration, wrapping him in warm, dry blankets, soothing, comforting, and healing him. But from there the psalm goes on to paint a very different picture:

> Yea, by thee I can crush a troop;
>   and by my God I can leap over a wall. . . .
> He trains my hands for war,
>   so that my arms can bend a bow of bronze. . . .
> I pursued my enemies and overtook them,
>   and did not turn back till they were consumed. . . .
> For thou didst gird me with strength for the battle;
>   thou didst make my assailants sink under me. . . .
> I beat them fine as dust before the wind;
>   I cast them out like the mire of the streets. . . .
>   (vv. 29, 34, 37, 39, 42)

This psalmist is no wilted, hopeless, thoroughly defeated victim. He turned to the Lord in his helplessness, and God gave him the power to go forth and fight his enemies until victory was won. God did draw him out from the swirling waters and deliver him from enemies who were too mighty for him; but he did it by giving the man a fighting spirit and the power to overcome the forces of evil.

Psalm 18 is a psalm of David; it gives an account of how God delivered the king from his enemies and made him victorious. It is also a messianic psalm, giving a prophetic account of Jesus' victory over evil. David was one of the mightiest fighters in all the Old Testament. You might protest that a psalm describing one of the mightiest kings and the Lord himself can't possibly be applied to a mere human being like you. Why not, son of God? Why not, daughter of God?

St. Paul was another man with a fighting spirit. Paul's letters give us the clear impression that he never hesitated to take on a person or an issue when confrontation was needed. He started out by vigorously persecuting the early Christians. After his conversion—in which the Lord treated him with about the same subtlety and reserve as Paul himself employed in dealing with others—he preached the gospel with tremendous boldness, confidence, and aggressiveness. He knew that the word of the cross was "the power of God," and he turned it loose without reserve or apology. With words that to many were folly and a stumbling block, he attacked the strongholds of the enemies of Christ. He had a great fighting spirit. He confronted the Jews in Damascus, Antioch, and Iconium. He provoked a wild riot at Ephesus. He deliberately stirred up violent dissension between the Pharisees and Sadducees when brought before the chief priests and council in Jerusalem for examination. He proclaimed the gospel to King Agrippa with such abandon that an incredulous governor, Festus, accused him of being mad. He was transported to Rome in chains, where he took on the Empire. Paul suffered imprisonment, beatings, stoning, shipwreck, hunger and thirst, cold and exposure, and many near brushes with death.

Paul wasn't able to endure all these trials because he was a stoic; he didn't have ice water in his veins. He was a well-formed, well-balanced, exceptionally gifted man of God who experienced the full range of normal emotional responses. He admitted to his experience of internal fear in his letter to the Corinthians (2 Cor 7:5). As a result of his trials in Asia he said, "We were so utterly, unbearably crushed that we despaired of life itself" (2 Cor 1:8). But he hastens to add that the effect of being so crushed was to make them rely all the more on God. Paul repeatedly spoke of his own weakness and the power which God provided him. He applied his fighting spirit not only to the preaching of the gospel but also to dealing with areas of weakness in his own life. Speaking about becoming Christlike, he wrote, "Not that I have already obtained this or am already perfect; but I press on to make it my own because Christ Jesus has made me his own" (Phil 3:12). And in 1 Corinthians 9:26-27 he said, "Well, I do not run aimlessly, I do not box as one beating the air; but I pommel my body and subdue it, lest after preaching to others I myself should be disqualified." He is actively applying the power of God to his own life, disciplining himself, fighting weaknesses, pressing on. Paul directed his disciple Timothy to approach life the same way: "This charge I commit to you, Timothy, my son, in accordance with the prophetic utterances which pointed to you, that inspired by them you may wage the good warfare, holding faith and a good conscience" (1 Tm 1:18-19). When the end of his days was in sight, Paul, who had so effectively overcome his fears and served the Lord with a fighting spirit, summarized his life with this stirring declaration: "I have fought the good fight, I have finished the race, I have kept the faith" (2 Tm 4:7). The Lord intends that same fighting spirit which led St. Paul and which Paul urged on his follower Timothy to fill the life of every Christian man and woman. Fear cannot stand before it.

The books in the Living as a Christian series can be used effectively in groups. To receive a free copy of the Leader's Guide to this book and the others in the series, write to Servant Book Express, Box 8617, Ann Arbor, Michigan 48107.

All of the titles in the Living as a Christian series are available at your bookstore or from:

Servant Publications
P.O. Box 8617
Ann Arbor, MI 48107

Send for our free catalog of Christian books, music, and cassettes.